Minority Invisibility

An Asian American Experience

Wei Sun

D1738993

UNIVERSITY PRESS OF AMERICA,® INC.
Lanham • Boulder • New York • Toronto • Plymouth, UK

Copyright © 2007 by
University Press of America,® Inc.
4501 Forbes Boulevard
Suite 200
Lanham, Maryland 20706
UPA Acquisitions Department (301) 459-3366

Estover Road
Plymouth PL6 7PY
United Kingdom

Library of Congress Control Number: 2007928243
ISBN-13: 978-0-7618-3780-0 (paperback : alk. paper)
ISBN-10: 0-7618-3780-9 (paperback : alk. paper)

Contents

Acknowledgments   v

Abstract   vii

1 Introduction   1
   Information Background   1
   Definition of "Minority Invisibility"   3
   Problem Statement   8
   Significance of the Study   8

2 Literature Review   10
   Historical Review of America Racial Formation   10
   Forms of Minority Invisibility   13
   Research on Asian American Study and Model Minority   20
   Theories Dealing with Invisibility   23

3 Research Procedures   25
   Qualitative Research Methods   25
   Recruitment of Participants   28
   Interview Questions   29
   Description of Participants   31

4 Data Analysis   33
   Individual Racial Consciousness   33
   Group Racial Consciousness   43
   Other Group Racial Consciousness   56
   Praxis   61

5 Discussion   66
       Discussion of Research Questions   66
       Implications and Future Research Directions   73

References   79

Index   85

About the Author   87

Acknowledgments

A few of my doctoral program colleagues at Howard University and I have presented research on the topic of "invisibility" at international, national and regional communication association conferences since 2000. I subsequently chose "minority invisibility" as the focus of my dissertation research and with the help and encouragement Howard University professors Dr. William J. Starosta, Dr. Melbourne S. Cummings, Dr. Richard L. Wright and Dr. Carolyn A. Stroman, I defended my dissertation, an early version of this manuscript, successfully. I also appreciate the support of Dr. Ronald L. Jackson, II, of Pennsylvania State University, who endorsed my dissertation and is my role model for scholarship.

My gratitude goes to my mentor and lifelong friend Dr. William Starosta, whom I have collaborated with since 1998. He guided me and trained me as a scholar. I owe each step of my academic growth to him. Kiran Starosta constantly listened and offered suggestions for my research and personal growth, especially as I struggled with my own invisibility. I cannot thank this couple enough for their encouragement and guidance.

Life is wonderful with the precious friendship of Dr. Andrew Jared Critchfield, The George Washington University and Dr. Sharnine Herbert, Shippensburg University of Pennsylvania. They have supported me over the past several years during my academic ups and downs.

I wish to acknowledge my colleagues in the Department of Communications at Bowie State University who support my scholarly efforts.

An article on "minority invisibility," based on data gathered for this dissertation, was previously published in *The Howard Journal of Communications*, a Taylor & Francis publication.

Finally, I thank University Press of America for making this humble manuscript visible in the academic fields of communication and identity studies research.

Abstract

Minority invisibility has gone unnoticed in communication discipline. It denies the existence of racial problems by consciously or unconsciously, deliberately or non-deliberately downplaying, ignoring or simplifying the problems. It is evidenced from the claims of color-blindness and reverse discrimination, the belief in model minorities, and exaggerated/negative/purposeful racial displays permeating American culture.

From in-depth interviews with fourteen Asian American professionals from various metropolitan areas, the current study investigates Asian American professionals' perceptions on minority invisibility and model minority status and explores Asian Americans' ethnic consciousness at four levels: (1) At a personal/individual level, how do Asian American professionals perceive their invisibility? (2) At a group/collective level, how do Asian American professionals perceive their ethnic group members' invisibility? (3) How do Asian American professionals perceive the invisibility of other U.S. American co-cultural groups? And (4) do Asian American professionals hold any expectation of changing minority invisibility in the United States?

After carefully examining the data collected from the interviews, thirty-four recurring themes were identified. The researcher then reduced these themes into four categories, and found out Asian American professionals have been acutely aware of a mainstream American culture. They view that different ethnic group members are in the relationship of co-culture to a mainstream. Invisibility is a subtle daily life experience for co-cultural group members, even for Asian American professionals. Diverse viewpoints on minority invisibility, model minority, satisfaction/dissatisfaction with mainstream American culture, and co-cultural ethnic relations are discussed in this study. They offer some suggestions for establishing a co-cultural coalition. Limitations and future research directions are indicated in the final chapter.

Chapter One

Introduction

INFORMATION BACKGROUND

Half a century back, in the prologue of his novel *Invisible Man*, Ralph Ellison (1952) narrated, "I am an invisible man...I am invisible, understand, simply because people refuse to see me." He then explains the "invisibility": "Nor is my invisibility exactly a matter of biochemical accident to my epidermis. That invisibility to which I refer occurs because of a peculiar disposition of the eyes of those with whom I come in contact. A matter of the construction of their inner eyes, those eyes with which they look through their physical eyes upon reality"(p.3). Ellison told a story of a young Black man's encounters from the South to New York Harlem in post-World War era America. Ellison spoke to many readers of color and recorded the feelings of rage in a racist culture. He believed that invisibility is a consequence of living within a white racist culture (Kim, 1997). Since then, "invisible man" has become a metaphor signifying the situation that persons of color, those negatively constructed group members' experience. Invisibility equates with voicelessness, being neglected, and silence within a mainstream culture.

Some social change has occurred since the Civil Rights movement, and co-cultural group members' conditions in American society have improved compared with the time when institutional racism distinguished a clear racial line between "white" and "colored." Within regulation of federal government laws, organized and institutional racism almost disappeared. However, co-cultural group members still experience discrimination in their lives. The difference now is that discrimination mostly takes subtle forms, making the fight with racism a more difficult task. Invisibility is such a subtle form of racism, it is not merely one ethnic group's experience, rather, it describes the partial

1

reality that various co-cultural group members face today. Reports from different co-cultural groups confirm the currency of the notion of minority invisibility: "a great many blacks" continue to think of themselves as victims of racism, inhabitants of "a fundamentally hostile, alien nation" (McWhorter, 2000, p. 213); African American men have been stereotyped throughout their everyday life experiences (Brown, 1965; Ellison, 1947; Jackson 2003& 1999; Orbe et al, 2000; and Wright, 1966). Invisibility in dominant white culture has challenged the African American male's self-affirmation and caused psychological distress (Franklin, 1999; Parham, 1999); Black feminists propose that the attention to African American male oppression has made African American women invisible; those African American women who are highly visible in popular culture have no voice (Wallace, 1990; Wyatt, 1999); and Native American scholars are invisible in mainstream American institutions (Lewis, 2003). Arab Americans are invisible in American culture at least until the September 11 2001 attacks on New York City's World Trade Center and Pentagon (Naber, 2000). Asian American professionals suffer negation of recognition for academic achievement and are under-appreciated (Kim, 1994; Ma, 1999). Asian Pacific American women struggle for visibility and voice in American institutions (Hune, 1998), and the like. Within a dominant white culture, co-cultural members' experiences are rendered invisible (Orbe, 1998; Samovar & Porter, 1994). These ethnic group members' voices are unheard, their needs are unfulfilled, and their self-identities are assailed. In a coming global communication era, it is necessary to raise the question of "minority invisibility" and to encourage the full participation of all persons in national and world cultures.

Asian Americans are a sizable population in the United States today. The U.S. Bureau of Census estimated that the total population of people of Asian descent was 12 million (4.3%) of the population in 2000. By 2049 the Asian population will (U. S. Bureau of the Census, 2000). According to a current survey conducted by Ong and Takanishi (1996), in 1996, Asian American adult population was 1,775,000. Among them, 24% were U. S. born, 33 % were naturalized, and 43 % were non-citizen foreign-born. Based on demographic profile of Asian descent population, Chan (2001) concludes that Asian American population is rapidly growing, ethnically diverse, possessing significant income diversity—from relatively high incomes to alarmingly low incomes. Asian Americans are largely foreign born, linguistically diverse, with many living in non-English environments; educationally diverse, with some groups at educational risk.

Asian Americans used to be excluded from citizenship, and were regarded as "foreigners within" and as "aliens." Asian Americans had been victimized by legal exclusion, disenfranchisement, and restrict enfranchisement (Lowe,

1998). Not until the post-world war era, in the 1960s, had the immigration policies considered to include Asian immigrants as "citizens." Since the 1980s, Asian Americans have been labeled the "model minority," as "honorary whites" (Liu, 1994; Tuan, 1999). Asian Americans are believed to enjoy success in education, rising income, a strong work ethic, and freedom from problems in mental health and crime (Lin, et al, 2005). Stereotypes of Asian Americans caused racial hostility or racial targeting. Model minority labeling serves as a double-edged sword that promotes racial dominance while silencing members of Asian ethnic groups. While the mainstream culture perceive Asian Americans as a trouble free "model minority," Asian Americans are still experiencing discrimination. The current study aims to investigate whether an active perception has developed among Asian American professionals. As "successful" examples of American culture, do they experience discrimination, unrealistic expectation, neglect, maltreatment or other identifiable treatment that differentiates them from the majority population? Do they have a community awareness? Is there anything they suggest to resolve the problem?

DEFINITION OF "MINORITY INVISIBILITY"

To define "minority invisibility," it is important to understand minority experiences in the United States, particularly how they form their identities within a dominant white culture. Min (1995) and Min and Kim (1999) illustrate two concepts with which minority identities are associated. Ethnic attachment is the term to measure the extent to which members of an ethnic group are culturally, socially, and psychologically attached to their own ethnic groups. Ethnic solidarity is another term to describe the degree to which ethnic members take collective action to protect their common interests (p.16). Min (1995) does not consider the possible development of attachment and solidarity with any group beyond one's own. He argues that a person is attached to his/her group culturally and socially when he/she identifies him/herself as a member of a particular ethnic group. With the awareness of ethnic identity, one will likely to participate in ethnic collective actions. Ethnic identity is key to both ethnic attachment and ethnic solidarity.

Until 1960s, the dominant paradigm in the study of ethnic relations in the U.S. was the assimilation model, assuming that all immigrant groups would achieve acculturation, social integration, and socioeconomic mobility after accommodating into the host culture. Researchers in the assimilation tradition tried to measure levels of assimilation over generations (Jewish, particularly the white European immigrant experience). However, since 1970s, cultural pluralism and ethnicity have emerged as research concerns.

Many theories of ethnicity can be classified into two contrasting perspectives: one approach regards that an ethnic or minority group whose members share many commonalities in physical characteristics, culture, religion, and historical origin is likely to maintain a higher level of ethnicity than other groups with fewer commonalities. In contrast, another approach rejects the assumption that ethnicity is determined largely by commonalities in physical and cultural characteristics and historical experiences shared by members of a group prior to migration. Instead, it offers the concept of "emergent ethnicity," the view that ethnicity is created and re-created in the context of adjustment in the host society. Thus it emphasizes residential segregation, occupational concentration, and other structural factors in the host society—including economic competition and the level of discrimination against the group—as the sources of ethnicity. Actually, the first approach explains ethnicity attachment, the second one explains ethnicity solidarity.

Min and Kim (1999) generalize three features of Asian American groups of the first perspective: (1) Contemporary Asian immigrants have brought with them distinctive cultural and religious traditions, for example, Chinese, Korean, Japanese and Vietnamese immigrants brought with them Confucianism and Buddhism. Indian and other South Asian immigrants transplanted at least three other non-Christian religions—Hinduism, Sikhism, and Islam. Because of the distinctiveness of their cultures and religions, contemporary Asian immigrants generally maintain a strong ethnic identity and a cultural boundary of ethnicity. But the second and later generations may have difficulty maintaining their parents' ethnic cultures and religions. (2) Asian immigrants have differing levels of cultural homogeneity. Korean immigrants have the highest level of homogeneity while Indian and Filipino groups are characterized by significant subgroup differences in culture and religion. This means Korean immigrants have advantages for maintaining ethnic solidarity over Filipino and Indian immigrants. (3) Since some Asian ethnic groups share more physical and cultural similarities than others, they can form a panethnic coalition more effectively than all Asian groups taken together (p.20).

Since the late 1970s, social scientists have put more emphasis on structural factors related to adjustments to the host society as the major resource of ethnicity than on the transplanted cultural heritage. Yancy, Ericksen and Juliani (1976) reject the traditional primordial approach (the first approach). They argue that the development and persistence of ethnicity is dependent upon structural conditions characterizing American social classes. In particular, they emphasize the ecology of occupations and residence as largely determining the development and persistence of ethnicity. In their view, the industrial and urban structures at the turn of the century made non-Protestant white immigrant groups more concentrated occupationally than the previous protestant immigrant groups. They argued that these non-Protestant (Jewish and Catholic) ethnic groups were able to develop higher levels of ethnicity not because of their cultural distinctiveness, but as a result of their occupational and residential concentration (Min and Kim, 1999, p.21).

Min and Kim argue that the formation of ethnic community (immigrant enclaves) is determined more by the group characteristics than by structural factors in American society. He illustrates that Chinese, Korean, and Vietnamese immigrants have established their own territorial communities, while Indian and Filipino immigrants are widely dispersed in suburban areas without establishing their own ghettos. Due to their linguistic-regional subgroup differences and lack of national identity, Indian and Filipino immigrants have disadvantages compared with East Asian immigrants in terms of organizing their territorial community (Min, 1995). On the other hand, Indian and Filipino immigrants, who represent higher socioeconomic status and more fluent in English than other Asian immigrant groups, may not need a ghetto. So these two groups lacked in group homogeneity, and were of a disadvantage in preserving native cultures and developing a national identity (Min, p.22).

There are two contrasting views on relationships of social economical occupation and ethnic solidarity. The first point of view promotes "reactive-ethnicity model," with belief that occupational concentration enhances ethnicity. When members of ethnic or minority groups concentrate in a few occupations, they tend to interact socially with co-ethnics, and feel a strong sense of group solidarity because of the overlap of their class and ethnic interest (Min, 1991; Yancy et al., 1976). The reactive-ethnicity model assumes that levels of ethnic solidarity have risen in modern industrial societies because industrialization has increased, rather than diffused, ethnic inequality. Modernization and industrialization have increased levels of contact with and competition among various ethnic populations for jobs, housing, and other scarce resources, which in turn has increased levels of ethnic mobilization.

To illustrate the above idea, some scholars constructed "middleman minority theory" (Bonacich, 1973; Wong, 1985; Zenner, 1991), which emphasizes the positive effects of a minority group's economic position on its solidarity. Middleman theory concentrates on small businesses, often distributing products made by the ruling group to minority customers (Indians in African, Chinese in South East Asia, Korean business in poor African American neighborhoods). Located in a vulnerable position between producers and consumers, middleman minorities encounter intergroup conflict with, and host hostility from, both groups. Middleman merchants' business-related intergroup conflicts and experiences with host hostility in turn have enhanced their solidarity. Korean experience in 1992 Los Angeles heightened Korean

Americans' political consciousness and second-generation Koreans' ethnic identity (Min, 23).

Opposing this, the "competition model" regards that ethnic groups with higher levels of assimilation are likely to show greater levels of ethnic awareness and mobilization compared to less-assimilated groups. Thus more assimilated members of an ethnic group also appear more likely to support ethnic movements (Olzak, 1983; Nagel, 1994). Michael Hecht and his colleagues proposed the idea of an "ethnic division of labor." According to them, ethnic solidarity is a reaction of a culturally distinctive minority group against economic exploitation by the dominant group. Reactive solidarity occurs when members of a culturally distinctive group are assigned to low-level occupations. Such members who are being exploited will use their ethnic collective actions to change the ethnic stratification system.

Minority members sometimes create new cultural patterns either to provide ethnic alternatives to dominant cultural patterns or to challenge them. However, this does not mean that some minority members can escape successfully from the negative effects of prejudice and discrimination. In the development of identity and self-esteem, all minority members are powerfully influenced by how they are perceived and treated by the dominant group. For some minority groups such as African Americans, their experiences with prejudice and discrimination largely determine their ethnic and racial identities.

For Asian immigrants, native culture brought with them from their home country may provide the main source of ethnicity. For second or later generations, a panethnicity is more likely to be identified. Although Asian Americans are now treated far more favorably than they were fifty years ago, as people of color they still encounter moderate levels of prejudice and discrimination. Despite of prevalence of the positive image, sense of no belonging (where are you from?), feelings of being strangers and aliens have negative impact on the psychological well being and identity of younger generations (Min and Kim,1999, p.34).

Gordon (1964) distinguished cultural assimilation and social assimilation. Cultural assimilation refers to the degree to which minority or immigrants members adopt the language, customs, and other cultural patterns of the host society. Social assimilation indicates the degree of their large-scale entrance into the institutions of the host society on the entry level. Gordon pointed out that a minority group could achieve a high level of cultural assimilation, but that such cultural assimilation does not guarantee a similarly high level of social assimilation because social assimilation requires acceptance by the dominant group. In other words, members of a group that has achieved a high level of acculturation can maintain a strong social ethnic attachment either because they are not accepted by members of dominant group or because they feel more comfortable interacting with co-ethnic members. Researches found out that Jewish and Japanese Americans display this tendency.

Studies show that some immigrants can achieve a high level of acculturation while maintaining their ethnic culture perfectly. Contemporary immigrants and children can maintain a strong bicultural orientation especially because of transnational ties to their home country. Latino and Asians maintain high levels of biculturality and binationality. Descendants of post-1965 immigrants have a strong bicultural and bilingual orientation.

Chang (2001) believes that Asian Americans have become increasingly visible in the political life of the country. Once relatively marginal, now they are quickly becoming elected officials, high-level political appointees, significant constituencies in elections, social party activists, campaign contributors, and influential policy advisers. Chang counted that by mid-2000, 300 Asian Pacific Americans had been elected to public office, and more than 2000 appointed officials at the state, federal, and territorial levels also are of Asian Pacific background.

Along with these achievements, interest in the voting power of Asian Americans has become commonplace, and Asian American voices have become prominent in many important social and public policy controversies, including in education, immigration reform, race relations and social policy. However, on a negative and ominous note, a national controversy with racial overtones erupted in 1996-1997 over alleged illegal Asian and Asian American campaign contributions and an illicit foreign influence on American politics. In 1999 a similar shadow loomed over the highly publicized (but false) accusations that Wen Ho Lee, a Chinese American physicist, had passed weapons secrets to the Chinese government. Thus the growing visibility of Asian Americans throughout American life has produced a new set of problems, along with unprecedented political opportunities.

Asian Americans are a fast growing racial/ethnic group. While a majority of this population is foreign-born, those with citizenship, either through nativity or naturalization, are becoming an influential force. The class and social positions of Asian Americans also have changed in recent years. The current Asian American population is much wealthier, better educated, and more diverse in occupation than before (Chang, 2001). Yet the number of Asian Americans in the lowest socioeconomic strata has grown as well. These demographic changes have expanded the possibilities for Asian American activism and influence, but also have contributed to the perception that they have distinct social identities and social problems.

Today's Asian Americans inherit a long and intense history of being the targets of racial injustice. They are in the midst of a rapidly evolving and complex contemporary racial environment.

The definition of minority invisibility is: minority invisibility denies the existence of racial problem by consciously or unconsciously, deliberately or non-deliberately overacting, ignoring or simplifying the problems. A few majority responses are: color blindness, claiming reverse discrimination, belief in a model minority, and exaggerated/negative/purposeful racial display, to name a few.

PROBLEM STATEMENT

As stated above, this study investigates whether an active perception has developed among Asian American professionals who have been in the United States for more than five years. Do even Asian American professionals experience discrimination, unrealistic expectation, neglect, maltreatment or other identifiable treatment that differentiates them from the majority population. The current study proposes following research questions:

RQ1: How do Asian American professionals describe their invisibility? How is this invisibility experienced and characterized by individual Asian Americans? How do they position themselves in a mainstream culture?

RQ2: How do Asian American professionals perceive their own ethnic group members' invisibility? To Asian ethnic group members, does invisibility promote survival or prevent their acculturation into the mainstream?

RQ3: How do Asian American professionals perceive the invisibility of other U. S. American groups? How is this invisibility experienced and characterized by selected groups?

RQ 4: Do Asian American professionals see any resolutions of changing minority invisibility in the United States?

SIGNIFICANCE OF THE STUDY

Minority invisibility has gone unnoticed in the communication discipline. It hampers the successful communication process in intercultural settings. Orbe (1998) regards "increasing visibility" as one important communicative behavior co-cultural group members employed in communicating with dominant group members (p. 78). Some co-cultural members already realized the importance of increased visibility. By exploring the issue of minority invisibility, this study explores contemporary Asian Americans' ethnic consciousness and interracial relations, and expands the view of intercultural communication by considering the possibilities of establishing co-cultural group coalitions. Chapter Two reviews literature on racial formations in the United

States, current studies on Asian Americans, and current theories on dealing with invisibility. Chapter Three discusses the research procedures of the study, theories to be employed in the investigation. Chapter Four displays data from interviews, and groups categories and themes of research findings. And finally, Chapter Five interprets the findings, addresses the research questions proposed in Chapter One, and discuss implications and direction of future study.

Chapter Two

Literature Review

Minority invisibility is a social phenomenon related to racial formations in the United States. This chapter offers a brief review of America racial formation and of current studies on Asian Americans.

HISTORICAL REVIEW OF AMERICA RACIAL FORMATION

Omi and Winant (1996) point out that the meaning of race is defined and contested through society in both collective action and personal practice. In the process, racial categories are formed, transformed, destroyed and re-formed. They use term "racial formation" to refer to the process by which social, economic and political forces determine the content and importance of racial categories, and by which they are in turn shaped by racial meanings. Racial meanings pervade US society, extending from the shaping of individual racial identities to the structuring of collective political action on the terrain of the state. At the micro-level, race is a matter of individuality, of the formation of identity, or of the ways in which people understand themselves and communicate with others. At the macro-level, race is a matter of collectivity, of the formation of social structures that are economic, political and cultural/ideological. Omi and Winant assert that the racial order is organized and enforced by the continuity and reciprocity between these two levels of social relations.

Omi and Winant argue (1996) that during each historical period, there exists a dominant racial theory, which "provides society 'common sense' about race, and with categories for the identification of individuals and groups in racial terms. Challenges to the dominant racial theory emerge when it fails adequately to explain the changing nature of race relations, or when the racial policies it prescribes are challenged by political movements seeking a different arrangement" (p. 11). Based on categories of ethnicity, race, and nation, the authors review three paradigmatic approaches to race and racial relations. They suggest that in the contemporary period, race and racial dynamics in the U. S. have been theoretically understood by relying on one or the other of three central categories: ethnicity, class or nation.

The dominant paradigm of race for the last half of 19th century has been that of ethnicity. Ethnicity theory emerged in the 1920s as a challenge to then predominant biologistic and social Darwinist conceptions of race. Securing predominance by World War II, it shaped academic thinking about race, guided public policy issues, and influenced popular "racial ideology" well into the mid-1960s.

Since the mid-1960s, dominant ethnicity theory has been challenged by class- and nation-based paradigms of race. These theoretical concepts challenge two central aspects of the ethnicity approach: first, from European immigrants' experiences came the conclusion that racial minorities could be incorporated into American life in the same way that white ethnic groups had been, and second, from white European experience came the belief that American institutions are fair and committed to quality and social justice for racial minorities.

In the late 1970s and 1980s, ethnicity theory met with "backlash" from white Americans. Although it sustained major attacks and required reformulation in certain respects, the dominant paradigm of ethnicity has not yet been supplanted. Ethnicity theory still remains a dominant paradigm.

However, Omi and Winant (1996) argue that ethnic group-, class-, and nation- based perspectives all neglect the specificity of race as an autonomous field of social conflict, political organization and cultural/ideological meaning. Each paradigm located the fundamental elements of race on their home ground (p. 48). For example, ethnicity theory focuses on the dynamics of incorporation of minority groups into the dominant society. This theory concerned questions of group identity, of the resolution of tensions between the twin pressures of assimilation (dissolution of group identity) and cultural pluralism (preservation of group identity), with the prospects for political integration via normal political channels. This theory best described European immigrants' experience in the United States. Thus certain apparent anomalies including the "success" of Japanese Americans can to some extent be addressed within the ethnicity framework. Writers within this paradigm note the frequent shifts of ethnic identity and political significance of its contingency, but fail to recognize the qualitative differences between white and non-white groups' encounters with the U.S. society. Or they fail to grasp the extent to which U.S. society is racially structured from top to bottom.

One the other hand, class theory believes that inequality of race is at the core of this assimilation theory. Class theory has been able to explain shifts in patterns of exploitation, mobility, and social control with great insight, but fails to notice the political and cultural dimensions of these shifts—often their most salient features.

Nation-based theory regards the real issue is not race, but national oppression and liberation. Race means a deeper national conflict (colonialism). The great insight of nation based approaches is their ability to connect U.S. conditions with global patterns based in the legacy of colonialism.

Based on the all three theories mentioned above, Omi and Winant present "racial formation": "the socio-historical process by which racial categories are created, inhabited, transformed and distroyed" (p. 55). Race is an element of social structure, "a concept which signifies and symbolizes social conflicts and interests by referring to different types of human bodies" (p. 55). Racial formation is a process of historically situated projects in which human bodies and social structures are represented and organized. Race is matter of both social structure and cultural representation.

> Our ability to interpret racial meanings depends on preconceived notions of a racialized social structure. We expect people to act out their apparent racial identities, we become disoriented when they do not. All racial stereotypes testified that a racialized social structure shapes racial experience and conditions meaning. (p.59)

Bob Blauner (quoted by Omi) considers there are two "languages" of race, one in which members of racial minorities, especially blacks, see the centrality of race in history and everyday experience, and another in which whites see race as "a peripheral, nonessential reality." Omi and Winant argue that since the earliest days of colonialism in North America, a racial order has linked the system of political rule to the racial classification of individuals and groups. The major institutions and social relationships of U.S. society-law, political organization, economic relationships, religion, cultural life, residential patterns, have been structures from the beginning by the racial order.

Racial minorities were always able to counterpose their own cultural traditions, their own forms of organization and identity, to the dehumanizing and enforced "invisibility" imposed by the majority society. They developed a strategy of "culture of resistance," using tradition, religion, family ties to sustain their own heritages (p. 80). Including the formation of ethnic communities. Cultural resources were nurtured among such communities, enormous labors were required to survive and to develop elements of an autonomy and opposition under such conditions.

In the present day, racial change is the product of the interactions of racially based social movements and the racial state. The postwar black movement later joined by other racially based minority movements, sought to transform dominant racial ideology in the U.S.. As a result of this challenge, the racial order anchored by the state was itself destabilized, and a comprehensive process of reform was initiated. Racial politics take place under conditions of "wars of position," in which minorities have achieved significant representation in the political system and in an ideological climate in which the meaning of racial equality can be debated, but the desirability of some form of equality is assumed. The new "rules of the game" thus contain both the legacy of movement efforts to rearticulate the meaning of race and to mobilize minorities politically on the basis of the new racial ideologies thus achieved, and the heritage of deep-seated racism and inequality.

Social movements create collective identity and collective subjectivity by offering their adherents a different view of themselves and their world. Disorganization of the dominant position and construction of an oppositional movement is a complex and uneven process, marked by considerable instability and tension. It involves not only reconceptualizing one's own racial identity, but a reformulating the meaning of race in general.

FORMS OF MINORITY INVISIBILITY

Minority invisibility takes subtle forms of color blindness, model minority, reverse discrimination, and "Otherness (marginalized)," silenced/muted group, and other.

Color Blindness

Carr (1997) argued that American constitution is "racist" and color blindness is a racist ideology (p. 107). In 1896, Justice John Marshal Harlan proposed: "But in view of the constitution, in the eyes of the law, there is in this country no superior, dominant, ruling class of citizens. There is no caste here. Our constitution is color-blind, and neither knows nor tolerates class among citizens. . . the destinies of the two races, in this country, are indissolubly linked together, and the interests of both require that the common government of all shall not permit the seeds of race hate to be planted under the sanction of law" (Harlan cited in Carr, 1997, p. 10).

Many whites believe that racism has effectively ended in American society, that America provides blacks as well as other minority groups with all the equal opportunities they need (D'Souza, 1995; Sykes, 1992). Jared Taylor even argues black racism is a greater problem than white racism. He compares Asians and Blacks in terms of perception, "if white racism were blighting the lives of black...should it not be a terrible obstacle for Asians as well?" Charles Sykes (1992) argues that racism has been emphasized overwhelmingly, even though white prejudice has declined and income for African Americans has increased. He claimed that it is time to put the charge of racism at rest. Harris (1994) finds out the different racial perceptions between white and minority people. Whites are convinced that minority by and large have equal opportunities, but a majority of blacks, Latinos and Asians rejected the idea that they have opportunities equal to those of whites (Cose, 1997). Cose points out that color blindness is the kind of silence that stems from apprehension about open acknowledgement of race. The attempts to ignore race only exaggerate its significance. Color blindness is a dream rather than a reality in contemporary America. It does not ensure the equality of white and non-white, on the contrary, it perpetuates certain racial problems. Cose (1997) proposes twelve steps to achieve a race-neutral society, which include: recognizing that race relations is not a zero-sum game, establishing interracial collaboration, looking for multiple solutions to racial problems, among others. In a survey study on color blindness, Carr (1997) finds out that 66% of African American students indicates that they are not color-blind when it came to race, while 77% of white students said they are color blind when it came to race Participants regard being color-blind means they do not discriminate and are not prejudiced or race means nothing to them (p. 149). There is a fundamental differences between white and non-white's perception on this term.

Two books, Arthur Jensen's (1973) *Educability and Group Differences*, and Richard Herrnstein and Charles Murray's (1994) *The Bell Curve* argued that the tendency of African Americans to score lower than whites on IQ tests is indicative of innate differences in intelligence between the two races. Liberals heaped scorn on the books, and conservatives did not want to be associated with them. Today evolutionary "racist" ideology cannot become the dominant, articulated ideology. An unknown number of people still believe in such a position but only a very few will openly subscribe to the ideology. Evolutionary racist ideology is incompatible with the new patterns of "race relations." Integration characterizes a significant part of the interaction between the white nation and nations of color. Nevertheless, national oppression and inequality continue, and if follows that ideologists would be hard at work constructing a new ideology concerning "race," which is color blindness. Denying the existence of the African American is not new, as has been shown, it was made an integral part of the constitution by the founding fathers. What is new is that it became the dominant ideology when it replaced evolutionary racist ideology. It was started in the 1950s as a liberal ideology promoted by integrationist elites. Then in 1970s, it was transformed into a conservative ideology using only part of Supreme court Justice Harlan's 1896 argument for a color-blind constitution.

The roots for color-blind ideology are found in the classic liberal doctrines of freedom—the freedom of individual created by the free capitalist marketplace. The difference between liberal and conservative is that liberals propose that government may intervene in some elements of the operation of the marketplace to make capitalism work better. Sometimes that means responding to the demands of the oppressed. Conservatives are opposed to most liberal efforts that would favor the oppressed. They claim government intervention is unconstitutional, immoral, and racist because the government is then not color-blind. They believe that government intervention actually makes the realization of a color blind society impossible.

Reverse Discrimination

Affirmative action has proved controversial. Beckwith and Jones (1997) offer that supporters of affirmative action argue that the history of discrimination against women and minorities in America has resulted in white males dominating and controlling the network of social society. In order to truly achieve justice and fairness the power base must be shifted in institutions. Affirmative action helps to achieve such equality. In the reverse case, people blame affirmative action as "reverse discrimination" which evolves into a system of racial quotas, timetables, and standards. Affirmative action is characterized as a compensatory remedy for past racial injustices or as a method for achieving racial balance in results. White males are largely hurt from affirmative action (Kuran, 1993).

Otherness (marginalized)

Scholars in postcolonial studies study the phenomenon of marginalization and "otherness" (Bhabha, 1994; Said, 1978 & 1993; Spivak, 1988). JanMohamed and Lloyd (1990) indicate that due to years of intellectuals' effort, a variety of minority voices have been able to question the dominant culture; however, dispersal of minority voices still produces fragmentation and marginalization, and such voices speak with little effect, since there is no function to the hegemonic culture and academic areas. JanMohamed and Lloyd (1990) assert that under the Western European-America domination in the academy, minority intellectuals play the role of "other." They are doubly problematic and twice marginalized in a mainstream system where they have to work. First, these minority intellectuals are cut off from their own cultures by being a part of Western hegemonizing institutions. Second, these minority intellectuals are marginalized within the institutions as the victims of continuing sexual or racial discrimination.

JanMohamed and Lloyd (1990) believe that minority discourse reflects the damage that the Western European-America hegemony does to minority cultures. The material destruction in social formation and economic formation affect the cultural formation, languages and identity of "minorized peoples." Their marginalization is legitimated. Minority cultures are regarded as underdeveloped, imperfect, childlike, inauthentic, perverse or criminal. The only way to elevate the low minority culture to a high level is through "assimilation."

Gupta and Chattopadhyaya (1998) present the concept of cultural otherness. Many people of industrially developed countries regard people of "underdeveloped" cultures as culturally inferior to them. Hallam and Street (2000) explore and analyze cultural encounters to expose a diversity of ways in which otherness has been constituted, communicated, and transformed in contemporary and historical contexts. "West and the rest" (p.1)

Cohen (1994) argues that anthropological writing tends to "deny cultural others a self consciousness which we so value in ourselves. There was an assumption that there is a difference between anthropological self and anthropologised other. A neglect of others' selves is an ethical issue which leads misrepresentation and should be addressed if the relationships between individuals and society are to be more adequately theorized" (Cohen, 1994, p. 56).

Understanding cross-cultural representation entails not only a self-reflexive and historical awareness of academic modes of production, but also an analysis of the ways in which 'other' have themselves translated and subverted "western" discourse. Without denying inequalities of power or the homogenizing tendencies of global processes, attention needs to be paid to the ways in which dominant representations are incorporated, resisted and reinvented.

Hallam and Street (2000) analyze the social, institutional and political relations which inform and constrain the meanings of cultural representations, tracing historical continuities and transformations. In doing so, they describe a diversity of cultural processes and encounters, highlighting the complex and polymorphous character of representations and cross-representations over time and space.

Jordanora (2000) thinks that notions of "otherness" can, however, be more widely applied, since the dynamic between self and other, at individual and at collective levels, is constitutive of all human relationships. Otherness serves as a constant reminder of difference.

Silenced/Muted Group

When Lee (1996) talks about discourses of exclusion, she feels that the voices of Asian America are absent, that in the United States discussions of race are generally framed in terms of blacks and whites, despite the fact that Asian Americans have been on the mainland of the U.S. for more than 150 years. Asians are still regarded as "strangers from a different shore" (Takaki, 1989) and voices from Asian America are excluded from the mainstream discourse on race. In some case Asian Americans are excluded because their high achievement.

Because of black and white discourse on race, most Americans do not view Asian Americans as legitimate racial minorities. Given this thinking, when institutions think about increasing racial diversity, they often focus on African Americans and sometimes on Latinos. Asians are largely absent from the discourse of diversity. For example, in constructing categories for minority scholarships and in recruiting minority students for admission, many universities exclude Chinese, Japanese, and Korean Americans. In her research on the controversy surrounding Asian Americans in higher education, Takagi (1992) found that Asian American students are at odds with university goals of diversity, in terms of either, and sometimes both, academic achievement and racial mix of the student body" (p. 81).

The reasons given for excluding Asian Americans perspectives from discussions of race fall into three categories. First, there are not enough Asian Americans to warrant consideration. Betty Waki, a Japanese American art teacher in the Houston Unified School District, was classified as white because the system did not recognize Asians as a racial category. Her racial status denied, Ms Waki subsequently lost her job because there were too many "white" teachers in the distinct (Omi, 1992). Second, Asians are perceived as unassimilable foreigners as opposed to American minorities. Oriental discourse holds that there are innate differences between the East and the West (Said, 1979). The quotation "Where are you from?" indicates an unwillingness to accept Asians as Americans. The image silences Asian Americans by denying them "the right to say anything except words of gratitude and praise about America" (E. H. Kim, 1993, p. 223). Asians are often seen as immigrants as opposed to minorities. Third, the model minority stereotype holds that Asians do not have any problems. In the minds of most Americans, minorities like African Americans, Latinos, Native Americans are minorities precisely because they experience disproportionate levels of poverty and educational underachievement. The model minority stereotype suggests that Asian Americans are "outwhiting whites" and have overcome discrimination to be more successful than whites.

Sleeter (1993) explains the relationships between Asian American and other minorities in the United States, that the media frequently connect African Americans and Latinos with social problems that many Americans regard as the result of moral depravity: drug use, teen pregnancy and unemployment. Asian Americans are hailed as the "model minority" portrayed as achieving success in the U. S. through hard work and family cohesiveness (Suzuki, 1980), following the same route to success that many whites believed their ancestors followed.

Thus, within the model minority discourse, Asian Americans represent the "good" race and African Americans represent the "bad" race. Asian Americans represent the hope and possibility of the American dream.

Lee (1996) argues that by describing Asian Americans as model minorities, the diverse and complex experiences of Asian Americans remain hidden. Instead of seeing different Asian ethnicities as being separate and distinct, the model minority stereotype lumps diverse Asian ethnicities into one racial/panethnic group. This representation silences the multiple voices of Asian Americans, thereby creating a monolithic monotone. In addition, by painting Asian Americans as a homogeneous group, the model minority stereotype erases ethnic, cultural, social-class, gender, language, sexual, generational, achievement and other differences. Furthermore, by describing Asian Americans as model minorities, the dominant group is imposing a categorical label on Asian Americans.

As put by Espiritu (1992):

An imposed category ignores subgroup boundaries, lumping together diverse peoples in a single, expanded "ethnic" framework. Individuals so categorized may have nothing in common except that which the categorizer uses to distinguish them. (p. 6)

The stereotype suggests that all Asians are the same because they all experience success. Thus the stereotype denies the poverty and illiteracy in Asian American communities(US Commission on Civil Rights, 1992). In addition to silencing the wide range of Asian American experiences, the stereotype silences the fact that Asian Americans experience racism (Chun, 1980; Kwong, 1987; Suzuki, 1980; Takaki, 1989).

As a hegemonic device, the model minority stereotype maintains the dominance of whites in the racial hierarchy by diverting attentions away from racial inequality and by setting standards for how minorities should behave (Kim, 1994; Lee, 1996; Sue, 1993).

In Lee's ethnographic study of the high school, she observes that white teachers, counselors, and administrators responded to evidence of racial imbalance/racial inequality by promoting the idea of equal opportunity. She warns that there is a significant gap between equal access and equal outcomes. She writes, "in urban areas, especially for low-income African Americans and Latino youths, public schools may offer everyone access in, but once inside the doors of public schools, many low-income youths are virtually disappeared" (p.24). Teachers of that high school believed their meritocratic system was fair, neutral, and color-blind. Unequal outcomes (i.e., high rate of African American student failure) were often silenced. When forced to face the reality of unequal outcomes, white teachers and administrators explained unequal outcomes as the natural result of differences in student talent, interest and effort (Lee, 1996, p84).

In Lee's study, white teachers and administrators suggested that the "success" of Asian American students served as evidence that the system was color-blind. In other words, "if Asians can succeed, then anyone can." Highlighting the achievements of Asians as a racial wedge in the debate in order to criticize institutions for favoring blacks at the expense of Asians and whites (p.120).

Omi and Winant (1996) note that merit is not neutral: "it is a political construct, by which employers, schools, state agencies, etc., legitimate the allocation of benefits to favored groups (i.e., organized), constituencies, and deny the validity of competing claims" (p.129).

Minority members learn to ignore the racism. In Lee's study, Asian-identified students were encouraged by their parents to work hard and ignore students who made derogatory comments regarding their ethnicity/race. According to Ogbu (1987), this attitude toward discrimination is typical of immigrant minorities. Ogbu (1991) writes, "they rationalize the prejudice and discrimination by saying as 'guests' in a foreign land they have no choice but to tolerate prejudice and discrimination (p.21). In Lee's study, Aisan- and Korean-identified students accepted that they were outsiders in the United States, and they understood that within the racial hierarchy they were beneath whites. Many blamed themselves for the discrimination they faced. They did not expect the dominant group to accommodate them but believed that they needed to make accommodations in order to gain acceptance. They did not speak about institutional or structural barriers.

Humor, self-mockery, and clowning are self protective and resistant strategies that racial minorities use to deal with the dominant group (Omi & Winant, 1986; Orbe, 1998). They are adaptations that the powerless group make to deal with the powerful prior to the politicization of the powerless (Omi & Winant, 1986). One consequence of this strategy is that those in power often come to expect self-effacing behavior from racial minorities.

RESEARCH ON ASIAN AMERICAN STUDIES
AND MODEL MINORITY

Asian Americans used to be excluded from citizenship, and were regarded as "foreigners within" and as "aliens." Asian Americans had been victimized by legal exclusion, disenfranchisement, and restrict enfranchisement (Lowe, 1998). Not until the post-world war era, in the 1960s had the immigration policies considered to include Asian immigrants as "citizens." Since the 1980s, Asian Americans have been labeled the "model minority," as honorary whites (Liu, 1998). Asian Americans are believed to enjoy success in education, rising income, a strong work ethic, and freedom from problems in mental health and crime (Lin, 1998). Stereotypes of Asian Americans caused racial hostility or racial targeting. Model minority labeling serves as a double-edged sword that promotes racial dominance while silencing members of Asian ethnic groups.

Lee (1996) reviewed how model minorities emerged and developed in a three decades from the 1960s to 1990s. The model minority stereotype emerged during the 1960s in the midst of the civil rights era. Critics of the stereotype argue that the press began to popularize the stereotype of Asians as model minorities in order to silence the charges of racial injustice being made by African Americans and other minorities (Osajima, 1988; Sue & Kitano, 1973). Prior to the period, Asian Americans had often been stereotyped as devious, inscrutable, unassimilable, and in other overtly negative ways.

Articles that chronicled the success of Asian Americans began to appear in the popular press in the mid-1960s. In December of 1966, *U.S. News & World Report* published an article lauding the success of Chinese Americans. The author wrote, "At a time when it is being proposed that hundreds of billions be spent to uplift Negroes an other minorities, the nation's 300,000 Chinese Americans are moving ahead on their own-with no help from anyone" ("Success story," 1966, p. 73). The article went on to praise the good citizenship of Chinese Americans and the safety of Chinatowns.

The prescriptive nature of the model minority stereotype is striking in this 1966 article. Chinese Americans were singled out as good citizens precisely because the status quo saw them as the quiet minority who did not actively challenge the existing system. That is to say, Chinese Americans and other Asian Americans were seen as model minorities because they were believed to be quiet/silent and hardworking people who achieved success without depending on the government. In reflecting on how Asian Americans have been characterized, Fillipina fiction writer Jessica Hagedorn (1993) writes, "in our perceived American character we are completely nonthreatening. We don't complain. We endure humiliation. We are almost inhuman in our patience. We never get angry" (pp. 22-23). Within the model minority discourse, "good" minorities, like "good" women, are silent (Cheung, 1993). "Good" minorities know their place within the system and do not challenge the existing system. *U.S. News & World Report* implied that other minority groups should model their behavior after Chinese Americans rather than spending their time protesting inequality. Thus Asian Americans were included in discussions of race in order to exclude/silence the voices of African Americans.

During 1980s, the model minority stereotype reached beyond Chinese and Japanese Americans to include Southeast Asians as well. Osajima (1980) analyzes the evolution of the model minority stereotype, asserting that even though the popular press began to recognize the potential negative implication of the model minority stereotype during 1980s, it continued to portray Asian Americans as exemplary minorities who gain success through sheer effort and determination. "New whiz kids: Why Asian Americans are doing so well, and what it costs them" (*Time*, August 31, 1987), lauded the academic achievement of Asian American students (Brand, 1987). It included stories of Southeast Asian refugees who overcame extreme obstacles to achieve academic success. In the author's words, "by almost every educational gauge, young Asian Americans are soaring" (p. 42). Once again, Asian Americans are depicted as brave, silent, and long-suffering people. The implicit message is that individual effort will be rewarded by success and that failure is the fate of those who do not adhere to the value of hard work.

The model minority stereotype of Asian Americans is alive and well in the 1990s. The popular press and public figures have continued to hold up examples of Asian American success as evidence that minorities can succeed in the United States (Hamamoto, 1992). Herrnstein and Murry's *The Bell Curve: Intelligence and Class Structure in American Life* (1994) once again casts Asian American as model minorities and African Americans as inferior. Asian American families have been singled out as examples of old-fashioned, tight-knit families. The stereotypic functional Asian American family is contrasted with the stereotypic dysfunctional black family headed by a single black mother on welfare. In his attack on political correctness and affirmative action programs, D'Souza (1995) argues that Asian Americans are a deserving minority being hurt by affirmative action programs. According to D'Souza, Asian American "success" is being punished, while African American or Latino "failure" is being rewarded.

During the 1992 riots that followed the Rodney King trial, the model minority image of Asian Americans was once again paraded across TV screens and newspaper headlines. This time Korean Americans were held up as legitimate victims who bravely sought to protect their private property. The conservative press represented Korean Americans as stand-ins for white, middle class America. Korean Americans were depicted as hardworking, self-made immigrants whose property was threatened by the unlawful anger of black America (Park, 1996).

In all of its permutations, the model minority stereotype has been used to support the status quo and the ideologies of meritocracy and individualism. Supporters of the model minority stereotype use Asian American success to delegitimize claims of inequality made by other racial minorities. According to the model minority stereotype discourse, Asian Americans prove that social mobility is possible for all those who are willing to work. Asian Americans are represented as examples of upward mobility through individual effort. Charges of racial inequality are met with stories of Asian American success, thereby reifying notions of equal opportunity and meritocracy (Chun, 1980; Hurh & Kim, 1989; and Johnson, 2000). Implicit in the argument that equal opportunity exists is the fact that the system is freed of any responsibility for inequality. According to this argument, if minorities (i.e., African Americans, Latinos) fail, they have only themselves to blame (Hurh and Kim, 1989).

A dominant majority was largely defined as a white European male Christian culture. Asian Americans who seek acceptance by the dominant group may try to emulate model minority behavior. In Lee's study in high school, many Asian Americans students willingly embrace the model minority stereotype. She argues that embracing the model minority representation is partially motivated by the fact that the characterization of Asian Americans as model minorities seems positive and even flattering when compared with the stereotype of other racial minorities. In that high school, Asian American students were always rewarded with teachers' praise and high grades for performing like model minorities. In their attempts to live up to the model minority standards, many Asian Americans students censured their own experiences and voices. Self-silencing and the uncritical acceptance of the model minority stereotype represent Asian American consent to hegemony.

The model minority stereotype takes attention off the white majority by pitting Asian Americans against African Americans. When Asian Americans and African Americans engage in interracial competition/tension, they are consenting to hegemony. While Asian Americans and African Americans are fighting among themselves, the racial barriers that limit Asian Americans and African Americans remain unchallenged. The resentment that the model minority stereotype engenders contributed to the racial tension in the 1992 riots in Los Angeles.

Chang (2001) and Gudykunst (2001) argues that the history of Asians in America can not be fully understood if they are not regarded both as immigrants and as members of nonwhite minority groups. As immigrants, many of their struggles resemble those that European immigrants have faced, but as people of nonwhite origins bearing distinct physical differences, they have been perceived as "perpetual foreigners" who can never be completely absorbed into American society and its body politic. To undergird their separateness, discriminatory laws and practices similar to those forced upon Native, African, and Latino Americans have likewise been imposed on Asian immigrants and their American-born progeny.

Chang (2001) further illustrated that the "acculturation process experienced by Asians in America has run along two tracks: even as they acquired the values and behavior of Euro-Americans, they simultaneously had to learn to accept their standing as racial minorities—people who, because of their skin color and physiognomy, were not allowed to enjoy the rights and privileges given acculturated European to survive in the United States, they had to learn to 'stay in their place' and to act with deference toward those of higher racial status" (p.211).

Both Chang (2001) and Gudykunst (2001) have acknowledged that Asian Americans have ambivalence status in American society: at one hand they are perceived as being successful in acculturation, and "model minority." But on the other hand, they are subject to continuing unfair treatment, including occasional outbursts of racially motivated violence.

Chan (1991) questions: will Asian Americans work alongside their multiethnic neighbors to bring about a more egalitarian society in the United States? Intrepid Asian immigrants have proven their ability to resist oppression and to survive. Whether or not Asian Americans can now become full participants in American life depends in part on their own willingness to channel some of their energies into public service—activities that improve the larger commonweal" (p.188).

THEORIES DEALING WITH INVISIBILITY

Scholars have approached the "invisibility" from different perspectives.

Dual Consciousness

W. E. B. Dubois (1910) offered "world culture" to resolve racial relations, as shared common African heritage, black and white should share one culture (Jackson, 1996).

Assimilation/Separation/Revolution

According to Peller (1995), integrationism comprises a set of attitudes and beliefs for perceiving the meaning of racist domination. Racism is related to ignorance. Prejudice based on skin color should be replaced by neutrality and treating people as individual.

Third Cultural Building

Starosta and associates (1995, 1998) suggest that by negotiating the cultural differences, dominant culture and co-cultural each renegotiate something and share some values in common; thereby an ideal interracial intercultural communication situation should be achieved.

Co-cultural Theory

Orbe (1998) believes that co-cultural group members tend to seek strategies to survive within the dominant culture. Avoidance, censoring self, using liaison, and increasing visibility are some of the strategies.

Ethno-relativism

Chen and Starosta (1998) claim that culture is ethnocentric by its nature. Ethnocentrism limits people from a full understanding of the human experience. Bennett (1986) develops an ethnocentrism model. It takes six steps from an ethnocentrism to ethno-relativism perspective: denial, defense, minimization, acceptance, adaptation, and integretion.

Existing literature does not lead to a resolution of "invisibility." This study will explore invisibility in four different levels: (1) at a personal/individual level, how does the individual perceive invisibility? (2) At a group/collective level, does the invisibility extend to a group of people or community? (3) How do co-cultural groups experience invisibility, and do they experience invisibility intertextually? (4) Do feelings of being invisible lead to praxis, and how?

Chapter Three

Research Procedures

This study investigates Asian Americans' ethnic experience in the United States, examines how "invisibility" affects their racial consciousness at four levels: (1) at an individual level, if "invisibility" is a problem to themselves; (2) at group level, how their ethnic group members deal with the problem of invisibility; (3) at the other group level, if they consider other ethnic group members to be invisible in American culture; and (4) if they offer suggestions for taking actions to change the current situation. Invisibility is a "received" view not one that can be counted by "neutral" third parties. Affected persons are differentially aware that what has happened to them has also happened to a class of other such persons. Those in a particular group are more or less aware of such formations. Some indeed, may not acknowledge them. In order to answer the research questions posed in Chapter One, this study blends grounded theory and intercultural listening methods as qualitative research methods and using in-depth interviews to collect and analyze information from fourteen Asian American professionals from various metropolitan areas of the United States. The current study studies Asian American professionals as an extreme case, as possible counter-examples to disconfirm invisibility, since if more "privileged" minorities experience invisibility, so will other groups.

QUALITATIVE RESEARCH METHODS

Qualitative Research Design

Numerous scholars in communication field have proposed the importance of qualitative research (Creswell, 1998; Denzin & Lincoln, 1994; Janesick,

1994; Lindlof, 1995). Creswell (1998) proposes that qualitative researches are unique in the following ways: qualitative researches emphasize process; they are interested in getting meanings from real people's real experiences; data are collected by the researcher rather than instrument; qualitative research involves fieldwork; and researchers and participants form a co-researcher relationship (Orbe, 2000; Orbe 1998). Qualitative research is descriptive and inductive. Janesick (1994) characterized qualitative design as holistic; looks at relationships within a system or culture; refers to the personal, fact-to-face, and immediate relationship; focusing on understanding of a given social setting; and not necessarily making predictions about that setting. It demands researcher stay in the setting over time, it demands that the researcher develop a model of what occurred in the social setting, and it incorporates informed consent decisions and is responsive to ethical concerns; and incorporates room for description of the role of the researcher and his/her bias and ideological preference. Finally it requires ongoing analysis of the data.

Grounded Theory

Glaser and Strauss (1967) define grounded theory as a "a general method of constant comparative analysis" (p. 273). In this method, theory could be generated from the data, then elaborated and modified. Researchers are free to fold previous research into the current one (Strauss and Corbin, 1990 & 1994). Like some other qualitative research, interview and field observation are the main sources of data collection for grounded theory. When the researcher collects, codes, analyzes and presents data, he/she should be able to interpret co-researchers' perspectives and voices. Researchers should take an active role in understanding what they observed, read or heard from the data. Categories should be drawn from the data and compared constantly.

Intercultural Listening

Based upon qualitative researches have experiences done in the field, Chen & Starosta (1998) develop a model of "intercultural listening" as a qualitative research method, viewing participants as "choice making" persons rather than as "object." They conclude that intercultural listening comprises ten procedures: (1) Adopting grounded theory, in which researchers listen attentively to the participants. (2) Bracketing assumptions, which means listening without inserting prejudices. (3) Gathering experience-rich accounts of stories participants tell. (4) Doing member checks when there is problem in the interpretation process. (5) Comparing what is said by participants across different contexts and situations. (6) Always leaving space for participants to say something new. (7) Asking for specialists' opinions for a double check on interpretations. (8) Believing that no conclusion is final in qualitative research. (9) Expecting the unexpected, and (10) Awaiting epiphanies.

In-depth Interview

In-depth interviews aim at understanding the complex behaviors and experiences of co-researchers in the social context (Fontana & Frey, 1994). By asking the same questions of all participants in roughly the same order, the researcher minimizes interviewer effects and achieves greater efficiency of information gathering. Such interviews developed from an attempt to make qualitative research more like a quantitative research. However in recent researches, in-depth interviews are used to study how individuals " read" the codes of ideology, class, gender, and race in popular texts (Lindlof, 1995). Each participant is an individual respondent. The researcher should generate and refine the interpretive categories in the process of data analysis.

In-depth interview process follows Kvale (1983)'s instruction on twelve aspects of the qualitative research interviewing situation.

1. Life-world. The interview focuses on themes which can better understand an interviewee's experiences and attitude.
2. Meaning. The interviewer registers and interprets interviewee's verbal and nonverbal messages, to make sense of what's said and how it is said.
3. Qualitative: The interviewer should get as much germane information as possible during the interview for subsequent analysis.
4. Descriptive: the interviewee describes in detail what s/he experiences and feels, how s/he acts. By collecting detailed materials and description, the interviewers may draw interpretations in a later stage of the research.
5. Specificity. Describes the specific situation and events in the interviewers' life.
6. Presuppositionless. The interview should not be a simple "yes" or "no" response. He/she should pay attention to the new and unexpected event during the interview.
7. Focused. Certain themes should be focused on during the interview.
8. Ambiguity. When an interviewee gives contradictory statements, the interviewer should clarify the reason the ambiguity occurs, and figure out what is really inside.

9. Change. It may be during an interview that an interviewee comes to change his or her descriptions of and meanings about a theme. The interviewee may not repeat the meanings he/she started with in the first interview, because he has obtained a new insight in, or an increased consciousness during the interview.
10. Sensitivity. The interviewer should have the ability to handle the topic he/she is not familiar with, and respect the cultural differences.
11. Interpersonal situation. In an interpersonal dynamic, the interviewer and interviewee react in relation to each other, and reciprocally influence each other.
12. Positive experience. A successful interview will enrich experience for both interviewer and interviewee.

Kvale (1983) also suggests possible phases of interview interpretation. First, the interviewee describes his/her life experiences; second, it allows the interviewee to discover new meanings during an interview; third, the interviewer may send the interpreted meaning back to the interviewee for double check; fourth, the interviewer interprets each interview independently before looking for commonalities.

RECRUITMENT OF PARTICIPANTS

A convenience sample is used to seek an Asian American perspective on minority invisibility and ethnic consciousness. This study is conducted within the legal and ethical guidelines of the Howard University Institutional Review Board. The participants are from a convenience sample, fourteen Asian American professionals who work or live in a metro area of the United States. The participants for this study are professional Asian Americans who currently work/live in a mainstream environment. They are adults, both males and females. The recruitment uses a "snowball" method following Lindolf's (1995) instruction. Taking the consideration that Asian Americans communication is more high-contextual oriented, and that Asian Americans would be reluctant to disclose issues to "strangers," they would most likely to speak their mind to a person they know well (Lee, 1992; Sun and Starosta, 2001). The recruitment of participants followed three principles: (1) Have been in the U.S. for at least 5 years; (2) live/work in a metropolitan area; and (3) work in a pre-dominantly white environment. The reason set the length of stay at 5 year is accordance with related immigration regulation, that a foreign born person can apply for citizenship upon five years' permanent residence. Following these criteria, the researcher identified a group of possible co-researchers among the people she knows who have a unique relation with various Asian American groups, briefly explained the project, and asked them to recommend other possible participants who fit the categories. By this way, the fourteen participants were located. The rapport between Asian American participants and the researcher is established through a third party. With permission of the Institutional Review Board at Howard University regarding the purpose of the study, the researcher conducts interviews to participants at a mutually convenient place. Multiple correspondences were employed in interviews. With face-to-face interview as the major method, telephone interviews and emails are also employed for follow-ups and member checks. They answered a fourteen item open-ended multiple set of questions. Thirteen interviews have been audio-recorded, upon the agreement of interviewees. The length of time for each interview varied from 30 minutes to 2 hours.

After getting data from participants, the researcher coded the transcriptions. The interview, data analysis and interpretation follows a blend of procedures discussed above, namely, grounded theory, intercultural listening, and in-depth interview. After carefully examining the information from transcriptions, the researcher addresses research questions from four levels, as proposed in previous section.

INTERVIEW QUESTIONS

The interview questions are designed to ask for the Asian American's experience and reaction toward minority invisibility; the questionnaire focuses on four levels of racial consciousness:

A. At individual level
  • Do you think there is a mainstream American culture? How do you see yourself in relationship to a mainstream American culture?
  • Have you ever experienced been ignored/neglected/invisible in America? Why did you feel that way? How did this make you feel? How did you deal with this?
  • Are you satisfied with your place in the American culture? If not, what would be better or fairer?
B. At group level
  • Have your ethnic group members been aware of a mainstream culture in America? How does your ethnic group relate to mainstream culture?
  • Have you ever seen your ethnic group members been ignored/neglected/invisible? How do they feel? How do they deal with the situation?

- Do you know the idea of "model minority"? What does this mean to you? What does that mean to your ethnic group?
- Do you think your ethnic group members are treated equally with their European American counterparts? How are they treated compared to African Americans?

C. At the other group level
  - How do other ethnic groups relate to American culture? Do persons of other ethnicities stand out as different from the U.S. mainstream?
  - Have you ever seen someone from another group be ignored/neglected/invisible? How do you feel about it?
  - What is the relationship between your own ethnic group and other such group(s)?

D. Praxis
  - Do you think invisibility/ignorance/neglect is a problem to you, to your ethnic group members, or only to other ethnic group members in the United States?
  - Do you see an answer to this problem to be something an individual person should do? Or persons of that ethnic community? Or all persons of many ethnicities in America who feel they are kept out of the mainstream?
  - Are there any other issues you want to discuss?

As soon as interviews have been done, the researcher transcribes the data from the recordings. After carefully reading the transcription, the researcher locates recurring themes from the proposed four categories. Under each category, various themes are collected from the responses. Chapter Four displays the themes and categories based on the interviews, and Chapter Five discusses the categories, and answer the research questions of Chapter One, which are:

RQ1: Do Asian Americans feel neglected/ignored/invisible in American culture? How do Asian Americans describe their invisibility? How is this invisibility experienced and characterized by individual Asian Americans? And how do they position themselves in a mainstream culture?

RQ2: How do Asian Americans perceive their ethnic group members' invisibility? To Asian ethnic group members, does invisibility promote survival or prevent their acculturation into the mainstream?

RQ3: How do Asian Americans perceive the invisibility of other U. S. American groups? How is this invisibility experienced and characterized by selected groups?

RQ 4: Do Asian Americans see any resolutions of changing minority invisibility in the United States?

DESCRIPTION OF PARTICIPANTS

The participants are from very diverse backgrounds, represent many professions, include members from nine Asian nationalities and come from Cambodia, China, India, Indonesia, Japan, Korea, Singapore, and Taiwan (China, Taiwan and Singapore are all Chinese descendents).

Fourteen Asian Americans from diverse backgrounds participated the study. They are from six Asian ethnic groups, Cambodian, Chinese, Indian, Indonesian, Japanese, and Korean. Among them, three were American-born, two emigrated to the United States at a very young age (one was two, another was 8), while all other nine were naturalized citizens. Six are females and eight are males. Thirteen of them possess at least college degrees. Their ages range from twenty-three to sixty. This study does not designed to determine how each different ethnic group of Asian descent reacted to "invisibility" in America. The researcher views Asian Americans as a whole community constituted of various groups from Asian ancestors. This study does not compare the differences of each Asian ethnic group, and thus does not offer each single Asian American group's problems of "invisibility," and does not distinguish how do they deal with it differently. The following table lists the demographic information of the interviewees, and each person was assigned a number to be addressed and discussed in Chapters Four and Five.

Table 3.1. **Demographic information of co-researchers**

Interviewees	Gender	Age	Ethnicity	Years in the U. S.	First language
I	Female	34	Indian	10	Malayalam
II	Female	23	Cambodian	21	English
III	Male	40	Japanese	32	Japanese
IV	Male	60	Korean	33	Korean
V	Male	38	Korean	38	English
VI	Male	26	Singapore	5	Chinese
VII	Male	38	Chinese	14	Chinese
VIII	Male	40	Chinese	13	Chinese
IX	Male	30	Chinese	6	Chinese
X	Male	27	Japanese	27	English
XI	Female	25	Korean-Japanese	25	English
XII	Female	34	Taiwanese	10	Chinese
XIII	Female	30	Indo-Chinese	30	English
XIV	Female	43	Chinese	8	Chinese

After getting information from participants, the researcher transcribes the interviews. After carefully examining the information from transcriptions, the researcher offers recurring themes under four categories: individual racial awareness, group consciousness, other group racial acknowledge, and praxis.

Chapter Four

Data Analysis

This chapter presents data on four levels of racial consciousness of Asian Americans to explore invisibility: (1) At a personal/individual level, how does the individual perceive invisibility? (2) At a group/collective level, does the invisibility extend to a group of people or community? (3) How do co-cultural groups experience invisibility, and do they experience invisibility intertextually? (4) Do feelings of being invisible lead to praxis, and how? Recurring themes will be collected under each of four questions. Actual words of the interviewees are quoted richly to support the findings. Categories are constructed from the recurring themes for further discussion.

INDIVIDUAL RACIAL CONSCIOUSNESS

At a personal/individual level, how does the individual perceive invisibility? The data analysis is based on three groups of categories: (1) Their relationship with mainstream American culture; (2) Their experiencing of invisibility; and (3) Their satisfaction with their place in American culture.

Three themes emerge regarding individual's relationship with mainstream American culture.

Theme One: Awareness of a mainstream American culture; feeling isolated from the mainstream American culture due to racial differences.

Seven interviewees indicate that they have been aware of a mainstream American culture. They confirm that they share the same value system with mainstream American culture, such as liking to work hard, pursuing higher education, and bonding to family, which are main factors for achieving assimilation into the mainstream working environment. However, they feel that their skin color and unique cultural backgrounds prevent them from fully being accepted by the mainstream culture. They have strong feelings of being strangers (Interviewee I, II, III, IV, VII, VIII, and XIII).

Interviewee I, an Indian American female professor, says:

> I see myself as different from mainstream America or rather middle, mainstream America – my color marks me differently. However, I do not entirely see myself fitting with any cultural group – I feel I am constantly negotiating with culture (Interviewee I).

Interviewee II, a Cambodian American who newly graduated from graduate school, feels that her Asian appearance distinguishes her from her European American colleagues:

> It varies, at times I feel no different from my Caucasian colleagues, however, in certain locations and situations it becomes obvious that my physical appearances do set me apart (Interviewee II).

Interviewee VII, a Chinese professional, expresses that he feels apart from mainstream culture, "I don't consider myself as deeply imbedded into the mainstream culture but there is evidence that part of my lifestyle conforms to the choices dictated by American culture." Interviewee VIII, a Chinese American engineer, and Interviewee XIII, an Indonesian artist, both feel that they do not belong to mainstream American culture, and their unique cultural backgrounds are not understood by their American associates.

While most interviewees regard that mainstream American culture represents white, male, European, and Christian culture, Interviewee X illustrates that "black and white" constitute the mainstream American culture. As an Asian American who grew up in Hawaii and now works in a metropolitan area, he feels he is an outsider:

> I do think there is a mainstream American culture, one that I think is "Black and White only." I think the "White" portion is the WASP centered one you can see on TV, a la Friends and the Gap commercials. I think it includes the whole "suburbs lifestyle" in which money is a vital part (i.e. must belong to upper-middle and upper class). However, I also think that there is a strong "Black" influence that can be found in the younger generations (i.e. teens, early twenties). It's that whole hip-hop and rap lifestyle that grew out of the "gangsta" image. By the

way, I only call it "black" because it appears (to me, at least) to have grown out of the rap and gang images portrayed largely through African-Americans (Interviewee X).

In talking about his status within a white-black culture, Interviewee X feels he is an outsider. He admits that he wants to be associate with the white part of the culture. However, as an Asian American, he can not find himself completely fitting into that image. He points out, "the fact that I may see my actions as 'trying to be white' causes me to step away from it. As a result, I feel like I don't fit into mainstream American culture. However, I don't really want to, either."

Theme Two: Awareness of and assimilation into a mainstream American culture

Four interviewees (Interviewees III, IV, IX, and XIV) also believe there is a mainstream American culture. However, rather than feeling different, they admire this multiculturalism, and have been, or are trying to embrace this culture. Interviewee XIV is still in the process of trying to understand this culture better so that she can assimilate into it well. Interviewee III believes that he has been "quite assimilated into this culture, mentally anyway" (Interviewee III). Interviewee IV assures there is a mainstream American culture, he comments:

> Multiculturalism is a beautiful thing of America. If you ask if there is a mainstream American culture, yes, there definitely is. All minority cultures emerge into mainstream. We feel it, it's powerful and it's very strong (Interviewee IV).

Interviewee IX recalled how he got the concept of mainstream culture, and how he dealt with it in his assimilation in the U.S. culture. Before coming to the United States, Interviewee IX has already heard that term "mainstream culture" from media continuously. He comments, "my understanding of mainstream culture is: Europeans came to the USA at early stages, whose languages, customs, values, food, religions have been formed into a predominate American culture. I think mainstream culture represents a positive, uplifting value of Western society. It doesn't have conflict with my birth culture—Chinese culture. I like to accept it, or I want to cooperate with them harmoniously." He believes harmony features of human beings, and regards the harmony is due to multicultural features of American culture. "America is a melting pot. I don't feel uncomfortable when dealing with a mainstream culture. I think it's perfect, nothing can be blamed about. I don't think there is flaw in it," said Interviewee IX.

Themes Three: "I" am the mainstream, whether people admit or not

Interestingly, two American born interviewees (Interviewees V and XI) claim that they are part of mainstream American culture, even though their American identity has been challenged because of their racial appearances:

> I used to think of myself as mainstream because I participate mainstream activities, I grow up as an American, speak standard English, and received education here. I live in a mainstream environment. However, I realize that people don't care what I care. When they look at your face, they define you as an Asian, as minority. This is the part I learn to remember (Interviewee V).

Similarly, Interviewee XI believes there is a mainstream American culture, and she sees herself as "immersed in the American culture, most entirely, due to the fact that I identify myself as being American."
Regarding an individual invisibility experience, four themes emerge.

Theme Four: Feeling of being invisible and visible at same time

Interviewee I describes a mixed feeling of being visible and invisible at the same time:

> Whenever I first join any "white" institution of group I experience both invisibility and visibility at the same time – while some people seem to be fascinated by my difference – others seem to avoid me. These experiences usually make me feel like an object – as though the others are viewing me as less than fully human or fully a person. I experience feelings of depression and frustration (Interviewee I).

Interviewee II shares the partial similarity with Interviewee I regarding "visibility," which leads to Theme Five, she feels that she stands out because of her racial appearance, not her personality.

Theme Five: Being visible because of racial appearance

Interviewee II describes how her racial appearance makes her highly visible in public: "I don't think I have personally experienced being ignored, rather the opposite, as a young Asian American female, I often find myself on the receiving endless of unwanted attention whether when I am alone, with my sisters, or with friends of other races, I notice many people staring at me. From women it often feels like they are sizing me up, especially other Asian women. From men, especially men of other races, it's unwanted sexual attention even when I am with male friends. It makes me uncomfortable, and makes me feel weak."

Theme Six: Invisibility is a daily experience: either it should be ignored, or it is an option, or a self feeling that the person should get over

Three interviewees recalled that in their childhood, they had experienced being invisible (Interviewee III, V, and XIII). With the passage of time, Interviewee III wonders if his memory was correct. He has learned to resist being ignored:

> I had been invisible and neglected when I was young, as in grade school. However this may not be very accurate due to my age at the time and my recollection. As an adult, I do get ignored. Such as when waiting in a crowd to be called upon to be assisted for something. They always pick someone who came later than I, but I don't see this as being ignored: I see those people as idiots (Interviewee III).

Interviewee IV, a Korean American who had being in the United States for more than three decades, admitted that during his life he has been invisible. But after he reasons the problem, he believes that being invisible is a choice and a privilege. As a first generation immigrant, he seems prepared for being invisible in American culture, and takes it for granted:

> Being invisible does not make me feel uncomfortable all the time. I am a very private person, and I like to be alone. Mostly it's my choice. I am very comfortable to be invisible. Most Americans like to speak their mind. That's not the way I want it. I am really invisible and private at the same time (Interviewee IV).

Feeling invisible since grade school, Interviewee V thinks that invisibility is a learning experience that he has to adjust to all the time. He recalled when he was a child, he had strong feelings of being ignored/neglected/invisible. Participated in an all white school, he was excluded out of white social circle simply because of his skin color. He sensed the change after growing up. "I feel less so as an adult. Ever since I went to university, I have learned to deal with the environment. People I socialize with, or work with are fine people. I don't feel so among them. Every once in a while I still have these kind of feelings. But I'll get over with it."

An episode that occurred between Interviewee VIII and the researcher before the interview was remarkable. When the latter contacted the former to set up an interview time, Interviewee VIII said that he is not invisible. In fact, he is very visible. But on the day of interview, he said he is invisible and told his story. As a Chinese American senior engineer of a renowned U.S. company, he recently was rejected for a promotion. He takes charge of responsibilities that a manager should do. But one of his European American colleagues who came later and who is less experienced was surprisingly promoted to the manager position instead. After unfruitful argument with the supervisor, he gave up the struggle. Interviewee VIII finally realized that it is not his performance that matters, it is the unsaid word "race." He said that in his company, those who hold management positions are absolutely whites. Minority members are merely taking mechanical responsibilities. The incident of his promotion makes him think about the racial problems in this culture more thoughtfully than before. Interviewee IX, a Chinese engineer, comments that in the United States, there exists a "glass ceiling" for minority employees. After certain level, they would never be allowed to be promoted into management level. The door has been closed to them to climb the higher positions.

When reasoning about this invisible experience, Interviewee VIII believes that lack of English communication skills is a fatal factor to stop his promotion. He told the researcher he had argued with the supervisor regarding the unfairness. He blames himself for not being good at interpersonal communication skills, otherwise "I would have pretended that I am happy, and thanked him for his goodness. Maybe things will be better." Interviewee VIII then recalls similar things had happened before, he had been rejected a promotion more than once. Each time the supervisor would pick on him, and pointing out his flaw in doing the job. " Finally we stuck there, and the relationship is ruined. I should have said, where do you think the problem is, can you guide me to the next level? Or appreciate his help. But I just couldn't say that flattery words. I think both of us should take responsibility for that"(Interviewee VIII).

Interviewee XII asserts that she is very invisible in America. She recalled that she used to work in a northern institution where the majority of residents are whites. She was the only Asian in that institution. Being young, Asian and single, she found herself never able to mingle with locals, who live within a Christian family tradition. She is always invisible. After five years' isolation in that all-white town, she moves to the west coast, where she could easily find her own ethnic community and other minority communities alike, and communicates easily. However, in her new institution, she found out that she has being paid much lower than an Asian male colleague of similar academic background. She suspects that being an Asian woman is a factor in this unfairness.

Interviewee IX regards that invisibility is an issue of personality rather than a social issue. He believes that invisibility is unavoidable to minority members. In his comments, if one minority could be able to assimilate into American culture well by speaking fluent English, making friends with people from mainstream, adjusting to their life style, and changing the hostile attitudes toward mainstream, things will be improved. The following conveys an extended sense:

Yes, I certainly have[experienced being invisible]. It's unavoidable. It depends on each person's personality, how do you understand it, and how sensitive you are. Feeling invisible always occurs to those people with high self-esteems. I think if you are open-minded, always look at the bright side of a thing, you won't take invisibility personally and negatively, it will go away (Interviewee IX).

Interviewee IX illustrate this idea from his own experience. When he first came to the United States, he has English language barriers. He often could not join in the conversation with Americans, because what they talked was typically mainstream culture oriented. He did not feel that he has been ignored by the mainstream. He also observes that Asian Americans do not involved politics in general, and never try to get what they disserved. Interviewee IX thinks that since Asian Americans are withdrawing from the mainstream, it's normal that they are ignored, that their voice is unheard. He says, "since you make no noise, the mainstream doesn't know your problem, so they do not touch your issues. You are ignored, un-valuable for them." He believes that both mainstream and minority should be responsible for this minority invisibility. Viewing minority's being ignored by the mainstream is not avoidable, he suggests minority members should participate in mainstream culture positively. By this way, minority would be able to draw attention on them. He is assertive in walking out of invisibility:

As to how to deal with invisibility, I think, for myself, I'll try my best to improve myself, to arm myself with knowledge, do it now, do it from myself. Be active. There is no way that mainstream will go to you, and the key point is you should try to involve in mainstream consciously. I am not saying that you have to "enter" the mainstream, but you have to be part of it. It's a necessity of survival. You live in a mainstream culture, at least you should be aware of it. When communicate with people, you should overcome the obstacle, be there, not an outsider. It's not good to separate yourself from the mainstream. Don't be self- isolated. I would learn more about American history and knowledge, improve myself, and enhance myself. That's basically what I do in dealing with this situation (Interviewee IX).

Interviewee VII is disappointed about being invisible in America. He regards that due to stereotypes and racial indifference, Asian Americans are treated unequally. He believes that negotiating with, rather than rebelling against to the mainstream culture would change the problem of minority invisibility:

I believe that sometimes because of racial indifference and stereotypes, sometimes Asians are treated unfairly. I feel badly of course but fortunately America is one of the few places in the world that allows people from every ethnic background to advance at least on the economic level with minimal prejudices. Basically human nature is to fear that which is different, and as time goes by, to be accepted by a society takes diligence, hard work, and diplomatic skills that will help the culture to absorb the ethnicity rather than rebel it. Make the culture proud and it will benefit all those associated with their advancements (Interviewee VII).

Interviewees X and XI both grew up in Hawaii in middle class Japanese American families, and moved to mainland United States as adults. They said that they did not feel neglected or being minorities until they moved to Seattle. Interviewee X said:

I do feel like I've been ignored and neglected, especially when I came to Seattle. Growing up in Hawaii, I was very much a part of the majority because Hawaii has so many Asians. So, when I became a minority at 18, I did feel out of place. There were some instances when I've experienced some outright racism, but it was more the feeling of just not belonging. I think it stemmed a lot from people not being able to relate to my experiences (Interviewee X).

Interviewee XI has a similar background. Growing up in a middle/upper class family in Honolulu, she was not aware of being ignored/neglected/invisible. However, after moving to Seattle, one incident changed her life. She was ignored in a restaurant and sensed the hostility toward Asians: "At the time it made me feel angry. In retrospect it made me feel like I should have spoke up more, been more active, and educated the people who I felt were being discriminatory."(Interviewee XI).

Regarding how to improve the problem of invisibility, Interviewees IV, VIII and XIV all suggest that minority members should work extra hard, to outdo European Americans so that they can stand out. Interviewee IV does not accept the excuse that minorities have less chance in USA. He argues that U.S. society believes in merit. He asserts, "believe me, if you are really excellent, the mainstream will come after you." Interviewee VIII also thinks that if he works twice as hard as his European American colleagues, he would be able to stand as equal. Interviewee XIV is actually doing so. Working in an adult educational institution, she establishes her professionalism and excellence by voluntarily working extra hours and brings unfinished work home.

Theme Seven: Invisibility has never been a problem for "myself"

Three interviewees (Interviewee VI, XIII, and XIV) said that they never experienced being invisible. Or it is just the other people's problem, not theirs. Interviewee VI said, " I haven't experienced such a syndrome of being invisible." Interviewee XIII specifies, "I don't think I am being invisible or ignored like many minority members in this country." Interviewee XIV said she has not been experienced being ignored/neglected/invisible in America yet.

In regard to satisfaction with their place in the United States, three themes emerge.

Theme Eight: I am satisfied with American culture

Six interviewees (Interviewee IV, VI, VIII, IX, XI and XIV) express their satisfaction with their places in American culture, and perceive American culture positively. The reasons for satisfaction vary: Interviewee VI appreciates the system to provide freedom; Interviewee VIII claims that he is satisfied with American culture generally, however, if the society could become more "sympathetic to the new immigrants," he would become more satisfied. Besides an expression of satisfaction, Interviewee IX insists that one has to improve him/herself to receive better treatment; and Interviewee XI, while satisfied with her own place in America, worries about the Asian Americans' well-being as a group in America:

Interviewee VI assures, "I'm quite satisfied with my place in American culture. I think this is one of the few places in the world where you can pretty much do what you want and when you want, short of breaking the law, and the level of individual freedom is liberating." Besides satisfied with his own places in American culture, Interviewee VIII would like to see people more sympathetic to the plight of the new immigrant. He said, "transplanting and learning a new language is quite a challenge by itself, but when coupled with racism and intolerance the burden can be overwhelming."

Interviewee IX does not think government should take responsibility for minority invisibility: "It's not deliberately systematic that government put you at an invisible place. It's yourself. To be better treated, you have to improve yourself."

Besides her own satisfaction with her own place in the American culture, Interviewee XI worries about Asian Americans' satisfaction in the American culture. She expects the society to stop stereotyping and discriminating against Asian ethnicities.

Theme Nine: I am not satisfied with American culture

Four interviewees (Interviewee II, III, X, and XII) express their dissatisfaction with American culture. Interviewee II thinks gender and race are the major issues for her unsatisfactory. She comments, "women have a hard time obtaining power, let alone Asian women...Unfortunately, Asians are often viewed as subservient, and therefore have a harder time achieving authority or influence in this society. I do not think things would be better until we can be viewed as equals with the other races, and more prevalent."

Interviewee III's dissatisfaction pointed to white males and Asian women, for ignoring him and other Asian males for getting a date: "I am not satisfied with my 'place' in this culture—especially in the geographic area that I live in. First of all, Asian males are the least favorite amongst the females in the social scene. Asian ladies prefer Caucasian men, Caucasian women prefer Caucasian men, and Caucasian men prefer Asian women. That leaves out the Asian men. This is not a race issue, however, nor is it a cultural issue. But it feels the same regardless."

Surprisingly, the complaint of Interviewee X's goes to "black and white issue only" phenomena. He thinks that African Americans have overshadowed Asian Americans. Not satisfied with him place in American culture, he gets tired of hearing white and black controversies. He would become happier "if people would recognize Asians as being a visible minority with all the problems and challenges that go along with it." He explains when it comes to racial profiling, the white press and black community leaders would admit that it is not only African-Americans being targeted, but that Asians experience a lot, too.

Theme Ten: My satisfaction or dissatisfaction with American culture depends on the experience at the moment.

The other four interviewees (Interviewees I, V, VIII, and XIII) admit that their satisfaction/dissatisfaction about American culture depends on situations. When everything seems all right, they are satisfied; but whenever they encounter the problems, or have been discriminated against, they feel much stressed and dissatisfied. Interviewee VIII is not satisfied because he did not receive the promotion which he thinks he deserve; Interviewee XIII actually is still wondering what her place is in American culture. Unless she finds a place to fit into American culture, she will not experience satisfaction.

Interviewees I explains her complicated feelings about her place in America. She says, "it depends on which day you ask me this question. However, on the whole I would say that I am somewhat satisfied. It also depends on which America you are referring to. Overall, I think that it would be better if people saw me more as an individual person rather than as a representative of a group, in my case Indian culture, thereby making all sorts of assumptions about me. On days that I experience discrimination and racism, I feel very angry and in a more global sense wish for an America that would be more tolerant and accepting of difference."

Interviewee V is hesitate to make the comment:

> Well (hesitate), hmm, it's a good question (chuckle). Am I satisfied with my place in the American culture? it's hard to say, my answer would be both yes and no. It really depends on circumstances and moods. Sometimes I feel very satisfied, but sometimes I feel I am not satisfied. It's hard to describe. Mainstream concept has been changing in the past decade. Take Latinos for example, they are part of mainstream culture now. Latino music has become a part of mainstream culture. It takes time (Interviewee V).

GROUP RACIAL CONSCIOUSNESS

At a group/collective level, does the invisibility extend to a group of people or community? Data analysis is based on four categories: (1) Group member's relation with mainstream American culture; (2) Group members' invisible experience; (3) Understanding of "Model Minority;" and (4) Compare Asian group's treatment with European Americans and African Americans.

From interviewees' perspectives, Asian Americans have been aware of a mainstream culture. Three themes emerge from the topic about group members' relationships with mainstream culture.

Theme Eleven: My ethnic group maintains a dual identity

Several interviewees (Interviewees I, III and XIV) regard their ethnic group members as having established a dual identity, which means while in the work place they readily mingle with mainstream culture; after hours, they reserve their own ethnic culture. Interviewee I comments that Indian Americans

> Vary much so [that my ethnic group members have been aware of a mainstream culture in America]. They usually respond by creating a dual identity – at work they try to "fit" in — but at home and in their private lives they retreat into their own community almost exclusively (interviewee I).

Interviewee XIV regards Chinese Americans' relationship with the mainstream depend on what backgrounds people have in China. He thinks at one hand most Chinese people have realized that they have to work really hard or harder than before to get themselves established. He observes, "partially people try to understand so-called mainstream culture, partially maintain one's own way if possible."

Theme Twelve: My ethnic group is isolated from the mainstream

Some interviewees worried that their ethnic groups are too apart from main-stream culture. Interviewee VII thinks his ethnic group (Chinese) members live outside the boundaries of the mainstream culture. He observes that more and more Chinese Americans have worked in all professions in the States, and that trade between China and U.S. has increased. Under this circumstance, Chinese Americans would become "an active member of the mainstream." Another Chinese American, Interviewee VIII, doubts the possibility of as-similating into American culture. He thinks mainstream media play important roles in communicating culture. However, since he and his Chinese fellows do not see much related to their culture, they simply choose to watch Chinese TV programs. He explains, "it's not the language problem. Basically because mainstream media only choose programs for their own taste, we want to watch Chinese-related culture programs. You can't find that from mainstream media. We always said, the mainstream media is biased. To know the truth, you have to watch both Chinese and American news, comparatively." He told the researcher that his Chinese friends mostly work in research institutes, universities, government, and in companies, they all feel it is difficult to melt with the mainstream. He observes that in the United States, even churches are separate. People of different ethnic backgrounds go to their own churches.

Interviewee II illustrated that Cambodian Americans are making an effort to preserve their own ethnic culture. However, she thinks that her ethnic group should try harder to get the mainstream to know them: "Cambodian Americans are aware of mainstream culture as they come into contact with it everyday. Many of my parents' friends work for the court system, airports, and hospitality positions. However, I have found that while trying to preserve our culture, many of our older generations cut themselves off from main-stream culture. We have our own societies to teach and practice reading and writing Cambodian language, dancing, and various traditions. I am not sure if I condone or oppose this, but I feel that our organizations should attempt to introduce mainstream culture into our own, rather than vice versa."

Theme Thirteen: My ethnic group is assimilated into the mainstream

It seems those who are younger, who came to the United State at a young age tend to assimilate into American culture, and take advantage of it. Intervie-wee V comments that in Korean community older generations are more sep-arate from the mainstream culture, while younger generations tend to assim-ilate into it. He regards age and educational background to all play important roles in choosing assimilation or not.

Interviewee IX, who came to the United States in his twenties, said that before he went to the United States, he had heard a lot about mainstream culture from Chinese media. He thinks that even if different, many cultures share common values. He listed the two opposites of relating to American culture: of assimilating into it at the expense of abandoning Chinese culture, which he had observed from American-born Chinese. Another is to keep Chinese culture while resisting of American culture. He comments that Chinese culture do not strongly adhere to American culture:

> Mainstream culture has no specific interest to Chinese culture. They don't regard Chinese culture as being positive. What they absorb is superficial, like Kong Fu, Feng Shui, they keep a general curiosity, politely (IX).

Interviewee III thinks that Japanese Americans are successful example of assimilation. Not only Japanese do accept mainstream culture, meanwhile, the mainstream knows Japanese culture better than other cultures. Interviewee X confirms this perception. He asserts that the 4th or 5th generation of Japanese-Americans have definitely been aware of the mainstream culture, they can relate to it fairly well: "If you had to pick an Asian-American group that was most assimilated, I think the Japanese American group would be one at the top of the list. However, I think the Japanese American community is able to maintain two worlds- fitting in to the white, middle-class American culture while keeping their Japanese-American one, too. Especially with the internment, the JACL (Japanese American Citizen League), the Japanese American National Museum, and so forth, I think there are many Japanese-Americans who see themselves as 'Japanese' and 'Americans.'"

Interviewee XI, a Korean Japanese American who associates herself with Asian Americans, thinks that Asian Americans are assimilated into mainstream in general:

> I see my ethnic group members as being Asian-American, as I come from Honolulu, Hawaii, there tends not to be any first generation Asians in my peers. And in this sense they are aware of mainstream culture as they are emerged in it and are a part of that culture (Interviewee XI).

Interviewee XIII is a second generation Indonesian American who does not speak the Indonesian language. She thinks the mainstream Americans do not understand cultural differences, and they disrespect people of other ethnic backgrounds. She seeks evidence from media, that media create stereotypes of minorities. Her wonder is that she is split between American culture and Indonesian culture: "This feeling is so weird that you are not belonging to any of the group, neither American, nor Indonesian. He [an Indonesian,

Interviewee XIII's friend] told a joke, if you know two languages, you are a bilingual; if you know three languages, you are a trilingual. But if you only know one language, you are American. Lot of Asians are very nice, they know their own cultures." Interviewee XIII thinks that Indonesians are aware of American mainstream American culture. All young people want to follow the trend. She worried that more and more people choose to assimilate into mainstream culture, the uniqueness of the Indonesian culture would vanish:

> Once I dated an Indonesian guy, he is so shamed about Indonesian culture. Whenever I asked him about Indonesian culture, he always said, why do you want to know Indonesian culture, it's countryside, it's backward, and you don't want it. He thinks he is part of American mainstream culture. Lot of people aware of who they are (Interviewee XIII).

In relating to ethnic group members' experiences of invisibility and how they deal with the invisibility, four themes emerge:

Theme Fourteen: My ethnic group members are invisible

Though three interviewees had said they have never been individually neglected, regarding their own ethnic group members' invisibility, all participants agree that their own ethnic group members are largely being neglected and ignored.

Interviewee I said that very often her ethnic group members are invisible and ignored. She recalled that when sometimes she and her friends dress in traditional Indian gowns in public places, they are served late and rudely.

Interviewee II has witnessed her parents being disrespected by white customers:

> I've witnessed my parents have been looked down on many times. My parents are shopkeepers in Northern Virginia, and while my father reads English very well, and my mother understands and speaks it well. I have witnessed American customers who come into their store with the attitude that they are somehow inferior because of their accents. Also, my father has a habit of bowing, which in our culture is a sign of respect, but I feel it makes the customer feel they have the power (Interviewee II).

Interviewee IV think that Asian Americans are invisible from American society, skin color matters. He realized that "being Asian is fundamentally different from being American, because of your skin color and your face. No one asks white European Americans where they come from. But if you are Asian, no matter how long have you been here, people would always ask you where are you from. Asian is a distinction. You look different, that's the way mainstream feels. They are confused, that's what I feel about the situation. Asian Americans are angry, and complain, but they cannot do anything about it. Surely they can write their opinions onto paper, but who will read it? Their neighbors won't care."

Interviewee VIII believes that Chinese Americans are invisible and neglected as well: "Many Chinese I know do technical jobs, they are invisible, I never saw them to go to conferences. Their managers get their data, and present like it's what they were doing. Many Chinese and other minority are exploited, invisible, and ignored. I don't know how do they feel about it."

Interviewee XIII knows that her mother, a first generation Indonesian American, has always been neglected. Other interviewees all provided the facts that they have witnessed their ethnic group members being invisible, neglected and ignored in America.

When asked about how do their ethnic group members deal with invisible experiences, three strategies emerges, which constituted the next three themes:

Theme Fifteen: Dealing with invisibility: striving for recognition

Some interviewees believe that each ethnic group should be responsible for its being invisible. Interviewee IX comments that "In the USA, one's social status is very important regarding how people treat you. If you have nothing to contribute to this society, no one will pay attention to you. Your education, your attitude, which means if you want to know mainstream culture, it's important for others to understand you. If you want to know this culture. It is hard to say that as an ethnic group, you are ignored totally. It does exist the cases that some members are ignored and invisible." But contradictorily, he also realizes there is an invisible ceiling for minority. "When you achieve a certain level, there is also a ceiling there to stop you get higher positions. It's common." He told a story of his friend who has been worked hard, been exploited, paid low. He was frustrated, depressed, disappointed, and got angry. Finally he brought a public attention to the matter, but quit the job he likes. Interviewee IX admits that most Chinese will not choose to do so. It is an extreme example. In most cases, Chinese would tolerate all the unfair treatment, or compromise. Sun and Starosta's (2001) study on expatriate Chinese conflict resolution has confirmed that in dealing with an intercultural conflict, Chinese prefer non-expression, tolerance, avoidance, self-forbearing, and compromise strategies. Maintaining harmonious interpersonal relationship, sojourner status confines, and cultural influences have all affect the way they dealing with the conflict.

Interviewee X saw his ethnic group members have been discriminated against, but he thinks it is an individual's choice how to deal with it:

> Some might put up a fight, some may remain quiet, while others try to "fit in." On a bigger scale, though, the Japanese American community rallied successfully for restituition, and because of the JACL (Japanese American Citizen League), I think the community would be able to "band together" if the need ever really arose. The fact that they have several Japanese-Americans in congress with influence (Daniel Inouye) helps them, too. The Japanese American World War II memorial that was built is an example (Interviewee X).

Interviewee VII also acknowledges that his ethnic group members are trying their best to assimilate into mainstream American culture, He said, "depending on the person and the position that they want in American society; some will migrate into professions that will give them more authority or influence. Some will strive for recognition in the social or economic arenas by educating themselves and ascending into the realm of the political elite."

Theme Sixteen: Resistance as a strategy to fight with invisibility

Interviewee XII, seeing two Chinese students were treated rudely by a European stuff, joined the complaint against this obvious discrimination. Interviewee I describes how her ethnic group members (Indian) deal with invisibility:

> They [Indian Americans] have been ignored very often. They usually feel and express a great deal of self righteous indignation. They deal with it by talking about these experiences in the community and criticizing mainstream America (Interviewee I).

Interviewee VI does not associate his ethnic group members because he has sensed that Singapore Chinese community only associate amongst themselves and "not really venture far out and assimilate into American culture" (Interviewee VI). As an assimilationist, he thinks being with a group resisting mainstream culture is an obstacle for him to achieve cultural parity.

Interviewee II observes that her parents developed their own strategy to rebel against the discrimination they received:

> I know that my parents do not like feeling disrespected, but at the same time, they do not rectify the situation. Rather, they smile to the customer's faces and

turn around and strike at them in their own language or get some satisfaction out of charging them more than their Asian customers (Interviewee II).

Theme Seventeen: Accepting invisibility as a part of life

However, most Asian Americans questioned would choose to be quiet, and accept the unfairness they received. Interviewee XIII said her mother, a first generation Indonesian American, accepted the fact that she should be ignored because of her dark skin:

> she accepts the fact [of being ignored, invisible] which I think is wrong, that she thinks she is a dark-skinned Asian person, which is not right, she thinks I can't change the world, just leave it alone. People behave differently according to the situation. Do you notice that Asian American are not showed on TV? (Interviewee XIII)

Interviewees IV and V both express that Korean Community have accepted invisibility submissively. Interviewee IV observes, "They (Korean Americans) are angry and complain, but they cannot do anything about it. Surely they can write their opinions into paper, but who will read it? Their neighbors won't care."

Interviewee V said that in general, Korean Americans have lack of voice in the United States. They have been aware of the seriousness, and have formed some organizations to solve the problem.

When asked about their understanding about the term of "model minority," what does that means to them as individuals and to their group members, among fourteen interviewees, only two of them have never heard of "model minority." One is Interviewee III, a Japanese American, and another is Interviewee XIII, a second generation Indonesian. All other twelve interviewees know this term. And they express two opposing viewpoints:

Theme Eighteen: Accepting "model minority" as a reward to hard working Asians

Interestingly, from the Interviewees' perception, they think many Asian communities tend to accept "model minority" term as a reward to hard working Asians. Interviewee I said that her Indian American community tend to live in this "myth." Interviewee II said that her Cambodian American community lives up the image. Like other Asian parents, Interviewee II has been pushed to be "child prodigy" all the way up to college. Her parents would always compare her with other Cambodian children, which brought high pressure on her personal growth. All her siblings were straight A students, they have been student body presidents, or gifted musicians. Her parents always push her to be the best for everything. Whenever she brought home a report card with a B, her parents would be disappointed. Even today, Interviewee II thinks this way:

> That is a lot of pressure to grow up with, and something I do not think my friends of other races ever had to deal with. When I graduated from high school, I was still a child mentally, and yet I went off to live at Virginia Tech under the most difficult major, Electrical Engineering, all because it was what was expected of me. Finally, all the pressure caught up to me, and I burnt out. I got tired of competing with all my parent's friend's children and even my siblings. I finally had to face the fact that I would not be happy trying to be this "model minority." After years of working various jobs, I've returned to school with a different mentality (Interviewee II).

Interviewees IV and V both recognize that some Korean Americans enjoyed the labeling of "model minority," while others regard it as a stereotype. Interviewee V distinguished the differences between old generation and young generation's reception of the term:

> They have impression that Asian students doing so well in school, Asian students making less trouble. Asians are family oriented, middle class, and they are less criminal. Asians are always compared with other minorities. It's a way to set up an example for other minorities. I think some Koreans are joyful for this term, and some others against it for this (Interviewee IV).

Interviewee V has a better understanding about "model minority" and he suggests that this term should not be used:

> Yes, I do know what means of "model minority." This term describes that Asian Americans are trouble free. They don't protest for unfairness, and they don't have a voice. But the "model minority" saying didn't get the whole story. It doesn't apply to the whole Asian American population. How does it mean to my ethnic group? Again it depends on whom have been asked for the opinion. The first generation of Korean Americans would regard it as a positive term, that's what they strive for. The second generation defines it as a limitation to the variety of Asians. They want to voice their political voices (Interviewee V).

Other interviewees present their understanding about the "model minority" as well. Interviewee VI admits that he does not know this term very well, but he does know that it related to Asians, "who are in general a minority in this country but are hardworking, intelligent and successful, relative to the other minorities who aren't" (Interviewee VI). Interviewee VIII receive "model minority" as an encouragement. He had heard about this term before he came to the United States. "I feel it's an encouragement. Like Michelle Kwan, etc, it's encouragement. If you are outstanding, you'll be recognized in American society. Even though ignorance and invisibility are problems if you are doing as good as your peers. As long as you are outstanding, you won't be ignored. For my ethnic group, like I said, what Americans can do, we can do also"(Interviewee VIII).

Interviewee XI objectively states what people understand about this term, "model minority is the stereotype that I see associated to all Asian ethnicities. To me as well as to my group this means that Asians and Asian-Americans are often held to a higher standard and/or misrepresented as those that achieve higher, are more intelligent, are more successful at math, have a more secure family and are thus the model minority."

Interviewee XIV extends "model minority" as a positive term from her own ethnic group members to all Asian Americans. She had read one article before in which stated that in the United States, students from Chinese, Singaporean, Korean, and some other Asian backgrounds achieve higher performance at schools, because they come from a culture emphasizing children's education. She also had read the reports on educational performance among different ethnic groups. It seems to her that Asian students are doing well in schools, in most subjects. She then comes to the conclusion, "I believe that American culture is based on equality for everyone. You'll have to compete with your own starting point. Sure, as a prosperous country in the world, the average American economic starting point is very high. But everyone is supposed to be offered the opportunity to climb the ladder at the current height. If you make progress upon your own foundation, it will be an accomplishment. I think "model minority" is a rewarding phrase"(Interviewee XIV).

Theme Nineteen: Regarding "model minority" as a negative stereotype

Even though they indicated their ethnic communities tend to accepted "model minority" as a positive term, some interviewees criticize this as a negative term that hurt Asian Americans at large, and demean other ethnic group members such as African Americans and Latino Americans in general. Interviewee I criticizes that by taking "model minority" as a positive term, it silenced inner community problems: "Yes, my community is haunted by the myth of a model minority. This leads to a silence in the community about issues such as domestic abuse, sexuality etc. We desperately want the mainstream culture to view us as successful and socially perfect whatever that means."

Interviewee II recalled that living up model minority image, she has been experienced personal stress in school at a very young age. She took AP class and her parents wanted her to leave high school a year early to attend college at 15. No one seemed to notice that she was a child who was attending classes with students 2 or 3 years older. She did not even learn to drive until she was in college, and it was practically inconceivable for her to have trouble in school. She recalled an episode, "once in my junior year, I was in an AP calculus class and academically struggling, when a Caucasian boy, a grade higher than me asked for my help on some problems I did not even understand. When I informed him of this, his response was, 'but, aren't you Asian?' To him it was so simple, but to me I felt like a failure."

Similarly with Interviewee II, Interviewee IV said that his daughters has been also bothered by this stereotype:

> One of my daughters said, she always got problems with this stereotype, because I am an Asian, should I be obligated to favoring math? Another daughter said, yeah, except when they are cheating. Being stereotyped like that, it's very ridiculous and funny. What does that mean to my ethnic group? Well, we are really becoming a model minority. We pay tax, commit less crimes, and formed a good community culture and neighborhood. I think media created model minority stereotype to set an example to other minorities. I really doubt what does model minority mean (Interviewee IV).

Interviewee VII disliked the labeling of the "model minority, " he regarded that Asian Americans "would feel bad but some may feel indifferent or apathetic and focus on the benefits that America has over the detriments." But he believes the image will help Asian Americans gain political power. Interviewee IX narrates how he knew this term and how he feels about it. He points out that by calling Asian Americans a "model minority," it implicates a devaluing of other minority group members, especially African American group:

> If I understand right, it's referring to all Asians. Besides Asians, there are a few minorities left, like African Americans and Latinos. The concept is: minority, but welcomed by mainstream culture; easy to be accepted. Asians' being called model minority is mainly because of low crime rate and avoidance of conflict. They only focus on work, not like African Americans, everything takes actions, and they have strong political consciousness. Asians are not demanding, they get low paid but work hard. It's a "condescend." When you praise one ethnic group, it devalues another. To ensure that you are welcome, but on the other side, it's unfair. To set an example, honorable white. Condescend. It's a from-up-to-down showing superiority. I didn't think about the term when I first heard it (Interviewee IX).

Interviewee X is also outraged toward this "model minority" labeling. He thinks that by setting up several successful examples of Asian American, it silenced Asian Americans voices in the United States: "I know the 'model minority' myth and I feel it is terrible. It pigeon-holes Asians into being the nerdy, science oriented and quiet image. As a result, I think a lot of Asians have to face glass-ceiling in the work place, suffer in school because they are expected to do well, and are not given the opportunity to explore the arts because people don't expect them to do such things. I mean, take away Jackie Chan and Jet Li, and how many Asians do you see on TV? And if you do [art major], there are always the 'nerdy' type or the 'seductive Asian female.' Asian Americans were not musicians, not artists, not loud and outgoing. Also, I think that image hurts a lot of the Asian youths, especially when their parents buy into that image and expect them to be doctors and engineers."

The following category investigates how the interviewee's ethnic group members compare their group with others. Do you think your ethnic group members are treated equally with their European American counterparts? How are they treated compared to African Americans, themes emerge.

Themes Twenty: Asian Americans are not treated equally with European Americans, but they have been treated better than other African Americans

Only one interviewee thinks that Asian Americans are treated equally with Europeans (Interviewee VI). However, he asserts that African Americans have not been treated as well as Asians. Ten Interviewees (Interviewees I, II, III, IV, V, VII, IX, XII, XIII, and XIV) acknowledge that European Americans have been on top of social status. They receive the best treatment in the United States. They get highly paid jobs, being awarded and promoted appropriately. They also admit that African Americans suffer most in this racist society. Asian Americans lie between white and black in this ladder-shaped social power structure.

Interviewee I argues that Asian Americans do not threaten the mainstream culture, that is the part of reasons Asian Americans have been treated fairer than African Americans:

My ethnic group members are not treated equally with European Americans. — from basic issues such as being paid less for the same job as their Euro-American counterparts to more subtle social and cultural issues. However, they are definitely treated better than African Americans — I think in part because we are not seen as threatening and there is no larger historical context that comes into play – of course South Asian New York cabbies are treated probably as badly as African-Americans (Interviewee I).

Interviewee II explained that in her multi-racial family, her parents were not respected by their Europeans in-laws:

> No, we are definitely treated differently than European Americans. Within my family, three of my sisters are married to Caucasians, one to a French man, one to a Jewish 'flower child,' and the third to a pure American 'mutt.' Each of the in-law families treats my parents and family members very differently. Which makes me wonder (Interviewee II).

Interviewee III indicates a fact how Asian Americans are treated better than African Americans:

> Asians are treated better than African Americans. You never hear about Asian drivers being pulled over routinely because they look suspicious, compared to what I hear about African Americans' experiences (Interviewee III).

Interviewee V specifies that media play a big role in providing biased images about minorities, he admits, "Definitely they are treated differently. Koreans Americans are perceived as outsiders, not part of American culture. African Americans are in the worst situation. Actually we are within the same category: minority. Media portray about Asians are always biased. For example, the case of Wen Ho Lee. Asian Americans' loyalty was suspected. African Americans do not relate to mainstream culture. They have their own notion of culture, art, music and other functions, and they live in their own reality."

When reasoning about the social phenomenon that Asian Americans' social status is lower than European Americans but higher than African Americans, Interviewees IV argues that Korean Americans have high social status when they are in Korea. But in the United States, they are treated as second class citizens. He thinks when more and more Asians enter professions, their social status will finally be enhanced. Interviewee I also indicates that many Indian Americans are among privileged classes in India. They are unhappy that they become minority members in the United States. Several Chinese Americans also agree that Chinese Americans divide into two extreme groups: one received high education in the U.S. and works in mainstream; another received less education in both Chinese and English and works mainly in Chinese-own businesses. Other Eastern Asian immigrants have never experienced discrimination based on race and skin color in their home countries.

Interviewee VII analyzes that Asian Americans' achievements have overshadowed African Americans:

> In most regions of the United States I would say Asian Americans are not treated equally with European American counterparts. In some aspects I would say that Chinese or Asian Americans have attained a certain level of achievement that

overshadows that of African Americans pertaining to the focus on education and economic aggressiveness giving them favor from some social classes of Americans (Interview VII).

Interviewee VII has also noticed that African American culture has influenced American mainstream in entertainment and sports. They gain more popularity than Asian Americans.

Interviewee IX confirms the perception that Asian Americans are treated worse that European but better than African Americans. He provided an outrageous example of how Asian Americans have been used to against African Americans in employment equality:

> I heard that when two persons compete for one position, even if their ability and contribution are the same, or even the minority is better, but finally the white will get promotion. I have an example. My friend applied for a job years ago, there were many other people applied for the position also. He was hired. After many years, in a very casual situation, the person who hired him said, "honestly, I do have racial awareness. When I consider candidates, I hired you but not blacks. Even though they are more experienced than you. It's for the consideration of my environmental safety." I think the message is clear. I was not in the situation. It's a most expressive one. Usually even you ask people deliberately about their opinions, they won't say it (Interviewee IX).

Theme Twenty-one: African Americans are treated equally as European Americans, or better than Asian Americans

Interviewees IV, VIII, and X believe that European Americans and African Americans are treated equally. Asian Americans are overshadowed by African Americans. Interviewee IV does not understand why African Americans feel unequal in the US society, since they have been assimilated into American culture:

> From my own experience and observation, I think they are treated equally. But from reading papers I know that African Americans are angry with the fact that Asian Americans are treated better than African Americans. I think it's awesome. Why? Because I think their ancestors were so acculturated into American culture, they learnt more and more about American culture (Interviewee IV).

Interviewee VIII acknowledges that European Americans always take advantages in promotion, and he gave an example that an African American woman was frequently promoted because she is a beneficiary of Affirmative Action. Interviewee X regards African Americans as overshadowing Asian males in media.

Especially Asian males who are asexual in the entertainment industry. We are definitely below African-Americans on the "cool" scale. I don't want to rant here so I'll just say that Asians are definitely less appealing than whites or blacks (Interviewee X).

OTHER GROUP RACIAL CONSCIOUSNESS

At other group level, how do co-cultural groups experience invisibility, and do they experience invisibility intertextually? Data analysis based on three categories: (1) other ethnic group members' relationship with mainstream culture; (2) Other group members' invisible experiences; and (3) relationship between interviewee's own ethnic group to other co-culture group(s).

In relating other ethnic group members' relationship with mainstream culture, two themes emerge.

Theme Twenty-two: Seeing other group members stand out different from mainstream culture

Six interviewees (Interviewee I, III, V, VI, VIII and IX) see other minority group members are very different from mainstream American culture. They point out color differences distinguish them from the mainstream. Each has his or her unique ethnic culture. Interviewee I says, "generally, most non white ethnic groups have a love-hate relationship with American culture – and yes they stand out as very different."

Interviewee III agrees that "other ethnic groups would be in the same situation, especially if they look different from Caucasians." Interviewee V regards Asian Americans, African Americans and Latino Americans are all minorities. He indicates that Latinos have slowly changed and they are gradually not outsiders in the U.S. any more. Interviewee VIII sees a relation among Asians, South Americans and African Americans:

It's similar with us. South Americans, black Americans are separated from mainstream. Each goes to their own church. Certainly some are integrated. Blacks are doing better than others. They stand up and are united to get attention from the society. We Asian Americans lack leadership (Interviewee VIII).

Interviewee IX specifies African American culture and Latino culture are different from mainstream culture. However, he detects that the mainstream tends to accept these cultures for their uniqueness. He thinks Asian cultures are less influential in mainstream America.

Theme Twenty-three: Seeing other group as similar to their own ethnic group (co-culture)

Many interviewees see all minority groups are naturally bonded because of their co-cultural characteristics. This allows them to stand on one side opposite the mainstream culture. Interviewee IV believes that as more and more minority group members are achieving success in the United States, that moves them closer to the mainstream. Interviewee II views the relationship of co-cultures as:

> I think that all minorities have a way to go before being as easily 'embraced' as Europeans/Caucasians. Blacks and Hispanics seem to be more noticeable in the media than Asians, but not by very much. In all ads or shows, there is usually one token of minority character (Interviewee II).

Interviewee XI thinks that every ethnic group as well as individual has their own way of relating to the American culture. Some cultures may stand out or have more difficulties in relating than others. Interviewee VII believes that every ethnic group will assimilated into the American culture according to their own specialized traits or due to their utilization by the mass population. Those with enough ingenuity will be able to leave a mark on society with some of their ethnic traits. Each ethnic group stands out until their characteristics are integrated and they can entertain a proportional amount of influence thereby transforming the mainstream into a minority based majority.

Interviewee X views other ethnic groups as "left out of mainstream American culture. They are invisible, too. I think that Asians are pretty far out there because of the way we look and for many of the newer immigrants, the fact that English is a second language for them" (Interviewee X). Interviewee XIII assumes that in bigger cities, it is easier for co-culture group members reaching out for each other. Interviewee XIV asserts:

> In a sense, it's true that each ethnic group retains, to an extent, its own culture, meantime, each tries to adjust to American culture (Interviewee XIV).

When were asked about other groups invisible experience, one sole theme emerges:

Theme Twenty-four: Other minority group members are invisible

Except for two interviewees who said they never saw other minority group members being invisible or neglected, the other twelve interviewees all state that they have seen other minority members being mistreated in the United States. Interviewee I has witnessed a mother and a daughter from South

America region being discriminated against and threatened, and the scene made her "feel outraged, angry and afraid" (Interviewee I). Interviewee II admits that whenever she saw other minority members were neglected, ignore, or charged with crime, she always tended to think from a mainstream way of thinking. And later she believes that "I feel each race is responsible for the views projected on them" (Interviewee II). Interviewee IV saw that other minorities have been invisible all the time, and he feels unhappy for that. Interviewee IV saw how people from different cultures who do not fit mainstream categories are blocked away from mainstream. While working for a mainstream institution, he has observed:

> While I witness that white and black colleagues work very well cooperatively. After work, they socialized with their own kind. Each leads a different social life (Interviewee IV).

Interviewee VIII adds to the evidence that how a minority members has been treated unfairly in his company. He tells a story of a South American who came to the company years ago. Many people hired by him got promoted but he stays in the same position for more than 2 years. Interviewee VIII says this colleague, "he came to the United States when he was 16. There is no problem for English communication. He always goes out with other minority members, even though he was promoted now, he is very late for that. We feel sorry for him." In the early session, Interviewee VIII has reasoned that his lack of communication skill prevented him for a promotion. He wondered with good communication skills, why his South American colleague could not get promotion either.

Interviewee IX, X, and XI all have noticed that minority members are ignored, neglected and invisible. Interviewee XIII recalled that when she was in grade schools, students from non-white backgrounds have had hard times, they also see that persons who are mistreated did not do anything. They feel angry regardless of the ethnicity of the person. Interviewee XIV admires Darwin's evolution theory. She asserts:

> Fitness survives. Whoever does well can survive. Otherwise, no matter which culture background he/she has to leave. In the Institute I work, I saw people leave, even European Americans, if they were not responsible for the job (Interviewee XIV).

Interviewee VII suggests not to evoke mainstream attention in case to receive more discrimination:

> Coming from a minority group one becomes hypersensitive to the discriminations that occur. Sympathetic to the minority, I sometimes force tolerance

towards the uneducated masses that repress these groups and focus on more positive ways to alter society. Sometimes criticism towards the masses can lead to further social isolation and resentment for a minority group (Interviewee VII).

When asked what is the relationship between your own ethnic group and other such group(s), four themes emerge:

Theme Twenty-five: Seeing one's ethnic group lack contact with other ethnic groups

Some participants see their ethnic groups lack contact with other co-cultural groups. Interviewee I indicates, "My ethnic group can be very racist – they tend to differentiate themselves from other groups and often see themselves as superior." Interviewee IX asserts that "generally speaking each ethnic group is separate within their own community. Even though I do have some friends with an interracial marriage. Most of my friends are from other minority groups, it's easier for us to understand each other. I would rather communicate with them."

Interviewee XIII does not see connections among Indonesian Americans and other minority members. She observes that members of each ethnic group would stay together, or try to get themselves a way into American culture.

Themes Twenty-six: My ethnic group and other ethnic groups are naturally bonded

Some participants see their ethnic groups and other ethnic groups are naturally bonded because they are all minorities. Interviewee II says, "I feel that within the Asian community, there is a unity on some level whether we are Cambodian, Vietnamese, or Chinese, etc.. However, on levels such as socioeconomic or academic there is some level of competition. Also, I feel there is a bit of mistrust of those who as different or deemed 'lower' than ourselves."

Interviewee III sees himself have good relationship with most ethnic groups. He believes he is not a racist. He only has likes and dislikes about other cultures, and they are racially linked. He feels that other minority groups have some common issues with different ethnic groups. Interviewee VI thinks Asian Americans get along with other groups easily. Interviewee XI observes that Asian Americans from different cultural/ethnic backgrounds are easier to associate with each other.

Theme Twenty-seven: Seeing self ethnic group and other ethnic group relations as competitive

Several participants see relations of their own ethnic group and other ethnic group as competitive. Interviewee VII believes that all co-cultural member "all share the commonality of disproportionate population within mainstream culture. Sometimes this commonality unites us in our quest for acceptance and sometimes it can bring dissension when one minority group excels more rapidly than another." Interviewee VIII asserts that a competition relation exists among minority groups, but he also admit it is easier to communicate with other minority members. He added, "even for kids at school, minorities go with minorities, they seldom go with whites. Even we have competition, we are friendly with each other" (Interviewee VIII).

Interviewee X explains the relationship between Japanese Americans and other Asian Americans. Japanese Americans see themselves as Japanese-Americans first, and then Asian-Americans next. In that sense, issues that have to deal with the newer Asian groups and refugees require a little outside prodding before the Japanese-American community will rally. He said, "I don't know the reason except for possibly the vast majority of the Japanese-American community were born and raised in the U.S. so they don't know the frustrations and challenges of coming to a new country. Thus, they may be torn a little between the 'American' view (i.e. Americans first!) and supporting fellow Asians."

Interviewee XIV see such relations among minority members as "mainly work relationship, friendly but competitive."

Theme Twenty-eight: Seeing own ethnic group and other ethnic group have a hostile relationship

Because of the 1992 Seattle Riot, two Korean Americans in this study see their group relationship with African American group as hostile. Interviewee V has sensed that the tension between African Americans and Korean Americans has always been a source of attention from the mainstream media. Interview IV says he read reports on conflicts between Korean merchants and African American customers in Metro areas sometimes. He says, "these are very isolated cases. But media played a big deal about it. They are some unfortunate cases between merchants and customers. But how many good customers, good relationships, and good neighbors of two cultures? I guess good relationships are always lot more than bad relationships. That's media's particular attention."

PRAXIS

The fourth level investigates if feelings of being invisible lead to praxis, and how it would be achieved. Data analysis is based on three categories: (1) whose problem is minority invisibility? (2) what is its resolution?

In answering questions do you think invisibility/ignorance/neglect is a problem to you, to your ethnic group members, or only to other ethnic group members in the United States? Several themes emerge from the analysis:

Theme Twenty-nine: Invisibility is a problem for everyone

Several participants regard that invisibility is a problem not only for individuals, but also for all the minority members in the United States (Interviewees I, II, XII, and IX). They think that Asian Americans should learn from African Americans who fight for civil right and racial equality. Interviewee II feel the mainstream media portray Asian Americans with stereotypes and prejudices. And that is something that all minority groups face regarding gender, races and sexual preferences. "Unfortunately I feel that Asians have not fought as hard as groups such as Blacks or Gays who have been more vocal and thus more widely seen," says Interviewee II.

Interviewee XIII also think invisibility is a problem to everybody. She complains people do not want to take time to understand other cultures. Interviewee XIV also agrees that "it is very hard to get mainstream culture to appreciate the cultural differences, let alone resolve the problem. I think that to understand and co-exist with the mainstream culture would be perfect." Interviewee XI predicts that "discrimination and ignorance probably will be a problem for a very long time. It is a problem for Asian Americans but even more so to other ethnic group members in the US."

Two interviewees regard that African Americans have drawn enough attention to the racial problems they encountered, that they expect more attention should be paid to other ethnic group members rather than merely "white and black issue" (Interviewees VIII and X). In Interviewee X's definition of mainstream American culture, it includes both European America and African America. He offers evidence from popular culture and media, and points out that in commercial advertising, the images of whites and blacks are dominant, only a few advertisings just put Asian face or Latino face for decoration or racial equality display.

Theme Thirty: Invisibility is subtle

Interviewee III thinks that invisibility is often done with subtleties, it makes the resolution very difficult. He said:

> I believe it exists a minority invisibility, and most of the time it may not be obvious. Invisibility and neglect is usually done with subtleties, so it's hard to detect. As for ignorance, you can't help it if people are not educated (Interviewee III).

Theme Thirty-one: Invisibility is a problem merely for other ethnic groups

Some participants (Interviewees IV and VII) believe that inivisibility is a problem merely for other ethnic group members, that their own ethnic group members have the ability to fully assimilate into the mainstream American culture by "hard working and economic sovereignty" (Interviewee VII). Interviewee IV praises that Koreans are very church-related people, and there is a strong community culture. He sees "many minorities have their own community cultures… and meanwhile, assimilate into mainstream culture."

Interviewee VII asserts, "I believe that it is less of a problem in my ethnic group because of our ability to adapt into the culture by means of hard working and economic sovereignty, some ethnic groups with less or no education and economic based social values face more difficulties. Isolation due to ethnicity is a problem for any group that assays to be part of the greater America."

Theme Thirty-two: Invisibility is merely a problem for my ethnic group members

Three interviewees (Interviewee I, V and VI) see invisibility is merely a problem for their own ethnic group members. Interviewee I thinks that "class, gender and sexuality make many people experience neglect and ignorance." Interviewee V specifies that "invisibility is not a problem for me personally. But it's a problem for my ethnic group members and other ethnic group members."

Interviewee VI denies that invisibility bothers him personally. He comments, "I think it doesn't affect me as an individual, as I haven't been a victim of poor treatment. I'm sure it happens to others. Perhaps less to Asians than to Blacks or Mexicans ."

Do you see an answer to this problem to be something an individual person should do? Or that person's ethnic community?   Or all persons of many ethnicities in America who feel they do not belong in the mainstream?

Theme Thirty-three: Resolving invisibility: it is important to establish coalition among co-culture groups

Most participants think that a coalition among minority groups should be formed in order to change the minority invisibility. Interviewee X comments that invisibility should be first fought by each minority community:

> Small changes have to come out by the actions of the individuals. Sure we can pass laws banning discrimination and such, but really, it is through the day-to-day interactions that makes a person stop seeing you as an Asian first and a person second (Interviewee X).

Interviewee I observes that her own ethnic group does not reach out enough to build and forge alliances. But she hopes that "all persons of many ethnicities in America who feel they are kept out of the mainstream should come together in a way that preserves and respects differences while simultaneously creating a sense of community."

Interviewee II suggests actions from Asian community to change media stereotypes about Asian Americans:

> I feel it is the responsibility to both the individual races as well as all minorities united. I think that the Asian community needs to realize that the problem exists before anything can be done about it (Interviewee II).

Interviewee II indicates that many young Asian Americans have not faced the same adversities as their parents' generation, and do not acknowledge the way Asian Americans are still being treated. She was told that her perceptions of Asians being negatively stereotyped in the media or other places are simply "over-reactions" and that she should just "lighten-up." She claims, "until Asians (as well as other races) can unite on the understanding that something needs to be done, nothing will ever be changed."

Interviewee III is optimistic about a formation of coalition between co-cultural groups. He foresees the importance of community actions: "An individual can only try to beat sense into the ignorant without getting beat up. A community can reach farther than an individual and with more backing. And if all communities of all ethnic groups are out educating, all we can do is wait for some intelligent, open-minded people to listen."

Interviewee V also acknowledges the importance of taking actions. He suggests the researcher to look at website of "Educated Voice for Korean Americans," a national association of Korean Americans, at www.cacdc.org, indicating that actions should be taken to fight with unfairness.

Interviewee VII believes that "everything must begin at the individual level. All ideas begin with one and eventually evolve into a substantial

movement. The ethnic community must become active at some level in order to achieve enough social impact for satisfactory results." He suggests
that every ethnic group should have their own agendas and goals to fulfill.
Seeing assimilation into the mainstream as a long process but a "tangible
task," he asserts it could be done if minority groups work together.

Interviewee X questions the fairness Asian Americans received. He con-
tinues to complain that "white and black issue" has overshadowed Asian
Americans. That "Asians are 'second-class' especially when it comes to having the mainstream community believe that we suffer problems, too." He
has been angered by the inequality of treatment and the numbness people accept it, and urges Asian American community unite to fight the unfairness. Interviewee XI believes education would help people realize the problems minority members have in the U.S. society. However, Interviewee XIII doubted
about the community action. "It's a huge task to change the world. It's not
personal decision. Just try at individual level, be proud of yourself," she suggests.

Theme Thirty-four: Self improvement as a way to resolve invisibility

Many interviewees (Interviewee IV, VI, VIII, and XIV) believe that self improvement is a way to change invisibility. Assimilation and educating the ignorant are suggestions from them. Many believe that if minority try twice as
harder, and work extra hard compared to European Americans, they will be
successful.

Interviewee IV believes in assimilation. He thinks Asian Americans mingle with mainstream Americans very fast, and he admires those successful
Asian Americans. He considers, "I do think if minorities work hard, they
could get what they want in this country. You have to respect yourself and be
successful. Believe me, if you are successful, the mainstream will chase after
you. I believe no pain no gain. The beauty of America is you can not blame
America that you don't have opportunity because you are minority. That's
bullshit. If you work twice harder, if you try harder than others, they'll come
and get you." He does not believe any complaints that minorities are left out.
He further illustrates, "The opportunity is there, you have to get it. If a minority comes and say, 'I didn't get promotion because I am a minority.' What
I will say is: 'You have to try twice harder.'" He believes those successful
Chinese, Japanese, Indians and Koreans have tried twice harder. He comments, "It's not fair, of course it's not fair. If you are mistreated, there are
laws. Opportunity is there, that's the beauty of America All minority should
try harder, it's land of opportunity."

Interviewee VIII regards enhancing individual's own quality is important for survival. "If you are outstanding, no one will ignore you. A white American could get promotion with an average ability. But for minority members, they have to be outstanding to be promoted. It's not fair, but that's the reality." He thinks expressiveness would be helpful in changing minority invisibility. He calls for a leadership to unite minorities together. And also hopes mainstream culture "should lower themselves, the America is an immigration country, and all members from different background come together to build for America a better society. If multiculturalism is taught from elementary schools, it'll be better off" (Interviewee VIII).

Interviewee XIV talks from her career, that immigrants should to be educated and work to make a living. One has to be involved in some activities in the communities. Take advantage of the free adult education programs in the country. Interviewee VI criticizes the person who is doing the ignoring. He also emphasizes the individual fitness:

> If you feel you have to prove yourself to someone for some reason, then do it. I personally feel that even though racism and bigotry run rampant, people are still judged on an individual basis...I say get over it, get on with your lives and not let people who don't matter affect the way you live in this world (Interviewee VI).

This chapter analyzed Asian Americans' racial consciousness from four levels, and distinguished thirty-four themes of how Asian Americans perceive themselves, their own ethnic group members, the other ethnic group members, and the possibility of changing minority invisibility. The next chapter interprets findings from Chapter Four, and addresses research questions that were offered in previous chapters.

Chapter Five

Discussion

Chapter Four presented data on four levels of racial consciousness of Asian Americans to explore invisibility: at a personal/individual level, at a group/collective level, at a co-cultural groups level, and at a possible level of praxis. Thirty-four recurring themes are collected under the above four categories. The current chapter returns to the research questions, reduces the thirty-four recurring themes into four categories, discusses implications regarding Asian Americans' relationship with the U.S. mainstream culture and with other co-cultures, interprets the underlying meanings of "invisibility," and compares and contrasts some themes across categories. This chapter also will discuss limitations of this research, and indicates future research directions.

DISCUSSION OF RESEARCH QUESTIONS

RQ1: How do Asian Americans describe their invisibility? How is this invisibility experienced and characterized by individual Asian Americans? How do they position themselves in a mainstream culture?

The first category investigates Asian Americans' individual racial consciousness, and tries to find out in what ways individual Asian Americans perceive invisibility. Based on findings of previous chapter, individual Asian American's relationships with mainstream American culture, their experiences of invisibility, and their satisfaction/dissatisfaction with their place in American culture are discussed.

Dimension 1: About mainstream culture

Themes One, Two and Three reflect participating Asian Americans' awareness of a mainstream American culture, and offers ways they relate themselves to this mainstream culture. For those who claim that they are isolated from the American culture, they believe that race, color and different cultural background distinguish them from their European associates, they feel powerless in view of this racial gap, and they choose to withdraw into their home bases— their own ethnic communities. Feelings of being strangers and of being rejected by the mainstream were commonly related. As Interviewee X described, the more he felt that he should assimilate into a "trying to be white" image, the more he was distanced from it. This experience makes him despair of ever fitting into mainstream culture. He felts like an outsider looking in. Other interviewees use words "not fitting" (interviewee I), "set apart"(Interviewee II), and not "deeply imbedded" (Interviewee VII) to describe their relationships with mainstream American culture.

When some of the Asian American participants recognized a line between themselves and the mainstream, some other Asian Americans, while being aware of a mainstream, are trying hard to assimilate into it. Some newly naturalized Asian Americans have acknowledged the existence of a mainstream prior to coming, and mentally prepared for joining the mainstream culture (Interviewees IX and XIV). For Interviewees III and IV, assimilation seems the only choice for survival. Interviewee IV is totally certain that all minority members will finally emerge into a mainstream that is "powerful" and "strong" in its ideological influence.

Theme Three, represented by two American-born Asian Americans, had believed or still believes that they are mainstream American culture. Interviewee V's belief has been challenged after he noticed that people judge him from his racial appearance, not the fact that he is an "American." Interestingly, they both believe that being "born in America" authorizes them to claim mainstream status.

Dimension 2: About personal invisibility

Themes Four to Seven discussed individual Asian Americans' experiences of invisibility. Three interviewees (Interviewees VI, XIII, and XIV) declare that they have never being experienced being invisible. Interviewee XIII implies that she is not like many minority members in this country, while others are invisible, she is not. Themes Four to Six classified different forms of invisibility. A majority of participants acknowledge that invisibility is what they experienced everyday (nine out of fourteen), whereas Interviewees I and II have sensed that their racial appearances is very conspicuous in American society. By being acutely visible, they are actually rendered invisible. Ironically, most of the participants regard that their invisibility in America is a personal shortcoming and therefore "unavoidable" (Interviewee IV). It is a communication skill problem (Interviewee VIII). Or it is a personality problem (Interviewee IX). They need to "get over it" (Interviewee V), improve it (Interviewee IX) or suppress it (Interviewee VIII). Interviewee VII regards that rebellion is not a solution for invisibility, because it would only cause further hatred and misunderstanding from the mainstream. Many interviewees suggest that by working extra hard and doing work that is twice as good as white Americans, they will finally bring Asian Americans to equality (Interviewee IV, VIII, IX, and XIV).

Dimension 3: About satisfaction/dissatisfaction with American culture

Themes Eight to Ten deal with Asian Americans' satisfaction/dissatisfaction about their places in American society. Those who are satisfied with their places in America are those who do not feel invisible (except Interviewee XIII), and those who take responsibility for feelings of minority invisibility (Interviewees IV, VIII, IX, and XIV). Those dissatisfied with their place in America (Interviewee II, III, X, and XII), criticize the American culture's general unfairness in gender and race. Interviewees I and V specified that personal experiences control their feelings and attitudes toward American culture at the moment.

RQ2: How do Asian Americans perceive their ethnic group members' invisibility? To Asian ethnic group members, does invisibility promote survival or prevent their acculturation into the mainstream?

The second category investigates Asian Americans' racial consciousness at a group level. Four themes based on findings of Chapter Four have been discussed: how the participants' ethnic group relates to mainstream American culture, group invisibility, reactions to "model minority," and comparisons to European and African Americans in equality of treatment.

Dimension 4: Group relationship with mainstream

Themes Eleven to Thirteen deal with how interviewee's community of Asian Americans relate to the mainstream as an ethnic group. No individual claims that his/her group belongs to the mainstream. Some participants view their ethnic groups as isolated from the mainstream culture (Interviewee VII-Singapore; Interviewee VIII-Chinese; and Interviewee II-Cambodian). Some participants view that their ethnic groups have been assimilated into the mainstream American culture (Interviewee III-Japanese; Interviewee V-Korean; Interviewee IX-Chinese; Interviewee XIII-Indonesian). And other participants specified that their ethnic group lies in between: instead of isolated from or assimilated into mainstream, they maintain a dual identity in America (Interviewee I-Indian; Interviewee III-Japanese; Interviewee XIV-Chinese). Assimilation is the strongest desire of the three. They observed that their own ethnic group members are distanced from the mainstream: Interviewees VII, VIII and IX criticized their own groups for being passive in emerging into the mainstream culture, but hope their group will finally achieve accommodation. Yet, they afraid that their group will be left behind. Feelings of powerlessness in front of a mainstream culture are commonly perceived. Each group has chose their own community as a home base, or has engaged in code-switching, working as they must with the mainstream, but returning to the sanctuary, their own community.

Dimension 5: Group invisibility

Interestingly, even though participants have different perceptions regarding individual invisibility, they all agree that their own ethnic groups are invisible (Theme Fourteen). From their understanding, their skin color and unique cultural background cause the problem. Three interviewees who declare they have never been invisible observed that their ethnic group members are invisible. The paradox of being visible as a person, but being invisible as a group needs to be considered in the last session of this chapter.

Themes Fifteen to Seventeen deal with how Asian Americans react to invisibility at a group level. Asian Americans as a group tend to be more critical of society, and more vocal. Though some of the interviewees consider their ethnic groups have accepted invisibility as a part of American experience, from the way they talk about it, they do not think that Asian Americans should have no voice or be accepting of their invisibility. Interviewee IV indicates that Korean Americans are feeling depressed but powerless about their invisibility. Interviewee V suggests all such invisible minorities should take collective action to solve the problem. Interviewee XIII regards that accepting invisibility as an unnegotiable part of life is wrong.

Suggested group actions toward increasing the visibility of Asian Americans, according to Themes Fifteen to Sixteen, are striving for recognition, choosing the path of assimilating into the mainstream; and resistance or fighting against perceived unfairness. While Interviewee XII joined her ethnic group members in a legal execution against discrimination, Interviewee I and II's group members chose passive resistance: they criticized American mainstream within the confines of their ethnic group community, or practiced a passive resistance. This is consistent with the strategies of conflict resolution disclosed for overseas Chinese by Sun and Starosta (2001).

Dimension 6: Model minority awareness

Themes Eighteen and Nineteen reveal how the Asian American respondents consider the idea of the "model minority." Most Asian Americans relate that their ethnic group members tend to accept the term "model minority" as a positive labeling for acknowledgment of Asian Americans' success in American culture (Interviewees I, II, IV, V, VIII, IX, and XIV). Especially the first generation immigrants tend to accept it as a "rewarding" from the mainstream. Many people try to live up the image. Interviewee II recalled that her parents and other Cambodian Americans would like do anything to keep this pride. But at a more personal level, half of the participants who do know the term "model minority" consider the term as a negative labeling (Interviewees I, II, IV, and VII), noting how it distances Asian American groups from other co-cultural groups such as African Americans and Latino Americans. The other half perceive it as an assurance and a confirmation from the mainstream. This finding is consistent with literature reviews on "model minority" in Chapter Two, that within a model minority stereotype discourse, Asian Americans are represented as examples of upward mobility through individual effort. Charges of racial inequality are met with stories of Asian American success by immigrants of color who are willing to work hard, thereby reifying notions of equal opportunity and meritocracy. The implication is that if other minority groups would only model their behavior after Asian Americans and restrain their protest against the mainstream system, they would succeed also (Chun, 1980; Hurh & Kim, 1989; and Johnson, 2000). This model minority image has been used to criticize blacks and Hispanics, thereby playing the communities against one another. The mainstream strategy may play on the strong Asian ego, the belief that it is possible to perform "twice as hard" as whites.

Dimension 7: Comparing treatment with Euro-and Afro- Americans

Themes Twenty and Twenty-one reveal in the eyes of the participating Asian Americans how social power is distributed. They rate European Americans at the top of the social ladder. Next in the power hierarchy is Asian Americans. Most participants acknowledged that African Americans and Latinos are at the bottom of the social order. Interviewee IX related an example of discrimination where a European employer hired an Asian American employee to keep two African Americans out of the competition. However, three participants assert that African Americans have received equal treatment with European Americans. For them, no improvement is needed. Interviewee X believes that Asian Americans are beneath African Americans in the social power distribution.

Arguably, invisibility is an obstacle for co-cultural members to fully enjoy the multiculturalism of America. Feelings of being isolated, different, not belonging, and not being able to fully assimilate into the mainstream have been haunting Asian Americans at large. For those who promote assimilation into the mainstream, only some individual successes have been reported; no group, as yet, has reached full assimilation. RQ3: How do Asian Americans perceive the invisibility of other U. S. American groups? How is this invisibility experienced and characterized by selected groups?

The third category discloses how Asian Americans perceive other minority groups in the United States. Based on findings of Chapter Four, three aspects are highlighted: how other minority groups appear to relate to the mainstream culture; what is the other group's invisibility experience; and do similarities appear regarding the participants' own ethnic groups and other co-cultural groups?

Dimension 8: Other ethnic group's relationship with mainstream

The Asian American respondents generally view other ethnic group members as non-mainstream (Theme Twenty-two). They believe other ethnic group members "stand out as different" (Interviewee I), "look different from Caucasians" (Interviewee III), and are "separate from mainstream" (Interviewee VIII). Similarities were found in the perceptions of one's own ethnic group and the other co-cultural groups' relationship with mainstream culture. From the participating Asian Americans' view, other ethnic group members are also "left out of mainstream American culture" (Interviewee X). Interviewee XIV indicates that even though each single ethnic group maintains its own ethnic community, they all aim to assimilate into mainstream culture. This is consistent with separation/assimilation perceptions of Asian American groups in category two.

Dimension 9: Invisibility of other ethnic groups

Like the observations made about one's own ethnic group, the respondents see other minority members to be largely invisible in American culture (Theme Twenty-three). Many participants have witnessed other co-cultural members being rendered invisible and being mistreated in America (Interviewees I, II, IV, VIII, IX, X, and XI). Interviewee VII explained that the fact of being co-cultural members of American culture somehow makes minority invisibility universal.

Dimension 10: Relationships with other group

Participating Asian Americans see four kinds of relationships regarding how their own ethnic group relates to other minority groups: (1) the other group is similar to their own ethnic group, are co-culturally or naturally bonded (Themes Twenty-four and Twenty- six); (2) one's own ethnic group lacks contact with other ethnic groups (Themes Twenty-five); (3) they view a competitive relationship between/among different ethnic groups (Theme Twenty seven); and (4) they sense a hostile relationship with certain ethnic groups (Theme Twenty eight).

In discussing the resolution of the invisibility, Interviewee VII regards that rebellion is not the solution of invisibility, since it only would cause hatred and misunderstanding from the mainstream. Many interviewees suggest that by working extra hard and doing twice better than white Americans they will finally bring Asian Americans to equality (Interviewees IV, VIII, IX, and XIV). As was said for one's own ethnic group invisibility, all participants admit most ethnic groups are invisible (Themes Fourteen). From their understanding, skin color and unique cultural background cause the problem.

RQ 4: Do Asian Americans see any resolution for changing minority invisibility in the United States?

The fourth category investigates the existence of invisibility and the possible resolution for perceived minority invisibility.

Dimension 11: Invisibility is subtle

Participating Asian Americans believe there exists a minority invisibility. Some see invisibility as a problem for everyone (Theme Twenty-nine, Interviewee I, II, IX and XII). Some see invisibility as only a problem for their own ethnic group members (Theme Thirty one), and some see it is a problem only for other ethnic groups (Theme Thirty one). As indicated by Interviewee III, that minority invisibility is subtle.

Dimension 12: Resolution for invisibility

The resolution for such a problem exists only in a utopia. However, many participants believe in the power of collective actions and coalitions among all such co-cultural groups, particularly among Asian groups (Themes Thirty Three). Some also suggest that co-cultural groups should use self improvement and finally assimilate into the mainstream as a final resolution for invisibility.

Few arguments have been made to challenge the mainstream. Mostly self-retrospection and self-improvement were advocated for Asian Americans. Proposals for establishing a coalition among co-culture groups are highly recommended. However, how to construct such a coalition is still in a conceptual stage.

IMPLICATIONS AND FUTURE RESEARCH DIRECTIONS

The previous session addressed the research questions within four categories. The following session discusses implications of the research.

Orbe (1998) defines dominant group members as "European American, male, heterosexual, able-bodies, and or from the middle or upper socioeconomic status" (p. 51). He argues that positioning of dominant or non-dominant status is contingent on co-cultural identities. He finds out that co-cultural members characterize their communication with dominant group members in consistent terms, for example, the co-cultural members uses terms "cautious," "careful," "fearful," "quiet," "uncomfortable" and "stifled" (p. 52). It appears, in communicating with mainstream culture, co-cultural group members consciously put themselves at a disadvantagous position. In seeking communication commonality with dominant group members, co-cultural members have to use strategies such like avoiding communication, maintaining interpersonal barriers between self and mainstream, making use of their intragroup networks for support, emphasizing commonalities, mirroring (or code switching), manipulating stereotypes, self-censoring, and extensive preparation.

Findings of the current research are largely consistent with what Orbe (1998) has found in his co-cultural study. Participating Asian Americans believed that all minority members in the United States have experienced invisibility in American culture. They have related their invisible experiences in detail. They have observed that members from their own ethnic groups have been ignored/neglected/invisible in dominant European American workplaces and daily life. They also indicate that other minority members are largely invisible in a mainstream American culture. Their strategies to deal with mainstream culture are within the existing co-cultural communication strategies: assimilation, accommodation and separation, though they also code-switching.

In research on Asian American communication, many studies have maintained an assimilation/adaptation focus within European American culture. Gudykunst (2001) distinguished similarities and differences for Asian American communication and European American communication. He indicated that Asian American communication differs from European American communication in ethnicity, cultural identity, generation, language ability, individualistic and collectivistic tendency, and shared ethnic network. He argued that Asian Americans who identify strongly with the U.S. culture might have similarities with European American culture, and tend to accept European communication rules. On the other hand, Asian Americans who do not identify strongly tend to communicate differently, and lack the motivation to adopt European American communication patterns. Rather than to permit equal co-existence, the mainstream culture calls for co-cultures to erase their difference and to become like them. Ironically, this they can never be permitted do (Starosta & Chen, 2003).

The current study finds out that Asian Americans have been aware of a mainstream culture. From their observation, they view that all other ethnic group members are in the relationship of co-culture to a mainstream. They are quite conscious of a dominant culture. Few challenges have been made by Asian Americans to such an existing dominant culture. Co-cultural group members tend to see themselves as submissive to a mainstream. This point is supported by how participating Asian Americans perceive themselves, their group members, and other group members in the shadow of a mainstream culture, and how to deal with such invisibility. As discussed earlier, participating Asian Americans blame themselves as being responsible for visibility in mainstream culture. Participants regard that their invisibility in America is a personal shortcoming and "unavoidable" (Interviewee IV). It is a communication skill problem (Interviewee VIII). Or it is a personality problem (Interviewee IX). They need to "get over it" (Interviewee V), improve it (Interviewee IX) or suppress it (Interviewee VIII). It is obvious that their thinking and their discourse are largely influenced by a dominant ideology. van Dijk (1993) talks about the relationship of elite discourse and racism formation. He indicates that political, media, educational, academic and corporate elites contribute to the formation of a persuasive dominant discourse. In regard to minority relations, such discourse is persuasive, wherein "speakers aim to influence the minds of their listeners or readers in such a way that the opinions or attitudes of the audience either become or remain close to those of the speaker or writer. In this way, speakers or writers may justify or legitimate specific cognitions or actions of themselves or other in-group members, or derogate those of out-group members" (p. 30).

By this mean, it is easier to understand why some participants of this study said that they are not invisible as individuals, but pointed out that their own ethnic group members and members of other ethnic groups are largely invisible in America; that invisibility is not a problem for their own ethnic group, but a problem for other such groups. Four implications could be drawn to explain this paradox:

First, participants might regard being ignored/neglected/invisible as harmful to their self-image. Denying invisibility would help to save face. The same rule applies to the superior feeling about one's own ethnic group. The image "my-group-is-doing-better-than-yours-in-America" brings one group closer to the mainstream but distances it from other co-cultures. To admit "model minority" as a rewarding term also reflects this self-protection, only this time at a level of saving group face, not just for individual face.

Second, the critical incident might not have happened to individual life yet that will sensitize the respondent and lead to a sense of futility. It is hard for individuals to imagine that they could become the victim of neglect/ignorance/invisibility. The best example is Interviewee VIII, before the incident of promotion, who thought his life in mainstream culture was quite positive, he was sure that he was quite visible in his working environment. But after his promotion was rejected, he started think more critically about his place in the mainstream culture. Interviewee IV, X, and XI used to think that being born in America, speaking standard English and assimilating into the mainstream differentiated them from other immigrant Asian Americans. They finally realized that in the eyes of the mainstream, they were not different from other Asians. Skin color and appearance matter. They have become suspicious of the system. In his newly published autobiography *My Country Versus Me*, the accused Chinese spy, nuclear scientist Wen Ho Lee (2001) recalled his experience in federal jails:

> In those isolated days being imprisoned, I always thought, the biggest mistake I ever made was that I came to the States to study for a doctorate. I must have done something wrong to disserve this mistreatment. I came to a sad conclusion: no matter how intelligent you are and how diligent you have worked, those Chinese Americans, Asian Americans who are like me, will never be accepted by American society. You are a foreigner forever. (quoted from *New World Times*, January 18, 2002)

From this sensitizing incident, Wen Ho Lee does not believe that the government would ever be fair to Asians. Asian Americans have a tendency to keep the problems within their community because of this mistrust of government.

Third, traditional cultural teaching may have taught Asian Americans to self-censor. As noted by many scholars of Asian American studies, Confucianism has been an influential ideology for East and Southeast Asians. Confucian doctrines including respect for authority, self-introspection whenever there is a problem, and modesty is a virtue make Asian Americans whose cultural heritage is from that region slow to blame the system for their mistreatment.

And fourth, from the experiences reflected at the level of individual, one's own ethnic group, and the other ethnic groups, invisibility is a subtle daily experience, it becomes a part of the fabric of the minority member's life. Ruth Chung, a young Korean American junior faculty tells her story as a Korean Americans in Min and Kim's (1999) book *Struggling for Ethnic Identity:* "I find I have to compensate for my race, gender, and age, and have to prove myself in ways that my fellow white, male, older colleagues do not. While they are automatically given a certain level of respect and authority, I have to earn every bit of mine" (p. 67). Her statement represents the Asian American professionals' voice in this country. Asian Americans are seeking a transformed identity in which traditional boundaries of race, gender, language, religion and culture have been mixed in a diverse American society, but they do not often do so openly, in the view of the mainstream.

Scholars have predicted that in the twenty-first century, co-cultural group members will occupy over half of the workplace (Blank & Slipp, 1994; Harris, 2000; Johnston & Packer, 1987). However, most of these employees are not expected to proportionately hold management positions. Those co-cultural members who have been promoted to management positions are usually overqualified, compared to European Americans (Harris, 2000). In Ancheta's (1998) study, quoted by Gudykunst (2001), after he distinguished several characteristics Asian Americans hold in common, he indicated that "Asian American's per capita income is below the national average, and poverty rates are higher than the national average. Despite these general tendencies, Archeta claims that Asian Americans generally are 'doing well' economically in the United States" (Gudykunst, 2001, p. 2). How ironic the statement is that Asian Americans are disproportionately poor but doing well economically in the United States at the same time. This fact indicates just like others in the present study that Asian American problems in the United States have been covered by a "model minority" labeling. Asian Americans are not being allowed voice and are largely invisible in this country.

Member checks were conducted after the previous interviews. The researcher presented findings from the research to several Asian Americans who fitted the original recruitment category. They were asked how do they think of Asian Americans' being invisible and is it possible for Asian Americans to assimilate into mainstream American culture. A few informants expressed that they have no clue other than they already provided. One informant reconfirms that living in the United States is a choice for each individual, especially for first generation Asian Americans. In order to be able to stand a chance in competition, minority members have to work extra hard to make a living. Upon being asked if it is fair for her to work twice as harder as her European Americans to stay even, she said it is not fair, but still she considers it is the only choice for her to survive in this country. "I believe no pain no gain. By doing so, I'll earn respect from my colleagues." She also believes that cultural differences might be a factor when people of different races do not mingle with each other. She offers that in the company she works, she sees her European American colleagues are also working hard. It seems to her that they do not have many social interactions with each other either. "I think it is still a cultural difference. That European Americans are individualistic oriented. On the contrast, we Asians like to be with friends all the time." Other than idealists who want to promote change, Asian Americans are more pragmatic oriented.

The findings of this study are accordance with research on middle class African Americans' perception on racial problems in the United States. McWhorter (2000) argues that even though African American conditions have been improved economically and socially in the past fifty years, a large number of middle class African Americans still feel the oppression and racism endanger their satisfaction with American culture. They are afraid that as long as racism exists, they will lose what they have. There is a fundamental difference on perceptions of racism between European Americans and co-cultural group members. The former believes that racism is over in the United States since civil right movement, and they do not experience what co-cultural group members experienced. They perceive racism as institutional prejudice. As long as racism is a part of structure of power, no matter how far a co-cultural member might progress socially and economically, he/she still experience racism. One's progress socially and economically does not make him/her immune from racism (Wright, 2002).

There is a commonality between middle class African Americans and Asian American professionals participated in this study. Asian Americans' success in American culture has been acknowledged largely, the participants in this study are well educated professionals. Even those who should be most shielded and most immune to difficulties of minority invisibility experienced it in every case either personally or at a group level. While they felt their situation was the same for some other minority group, they mostly avoided action or considered action appropriate only for Asian Americans. The study could not disconfirm, even for those who seem the best off in class and language proficiency, "positive" stereotype, and denials of racism.

The current study suggests four level of Asian American racial consciousness training model: Co-cultural group members should be aware of their individual racial identity, their own ethnic group identity, their co-cultural identity, and finally, they should seek coalitions with other co-cultural groups including non-Asians to make America a better place.

This study investigates Asian American ethnic consciousness and perceptions about minority invisibility on four levels: individual, group, other group and praxis. These four levels have been used to guide further analysis. It addresses research questions such: How do Asian Americans describe their invisibility? How is this invisibility experienced and characterized by individual Asian Americans? How do they position themselves in a mainstream culture? How do Asian Americans perceive their ethnic group members' invisibility? How is this group invisibility formation advanced? To Asian ethnic group members, does invisibility promote survival or prevent their acculturation into the mainstream? How do Asian Americans perceive the invisibility of other U. S. American groups? How is this invisibility experienced and characterized by selected groups? Do Asian Americans see any resolutions of changing minority invisibility in the United States? Few studies have attempted answers to those questions in intercultural/interracial communication research. The findings of this research support the co-cultural predictions and expands them.

The limitation of this study is that class element among Asian Americans has not been taken consideration. Among fourteen participants, only one respondent is not college educated. The invisibility experiences examined in this study are mainly middle or upper Asian Americans. Asian Americans of the poor, the non-English literate, and those who live in ghettos have been eliminated from the study.

Future research should expand the study to a diverse population of Asian Americans, for example, what differences are perceived regarding invisibility for those for whom English serves as a first language versus those for whom it does not? How do social, economic, and educational factors affect their assimilation into mainstream? Does foreignness of features have a differential impact on Asian Americans from different geographical regions? More importantly, how do other ethnic group members perceive invisibility? How do other ethnic group members perceive Asian Americans in relationship to the mainstream American culture? Do they see a unified solution for minority invisibility? Is a coalition among co-cultural groups possible, and how?

References

Ancheta, A. (1998). *Race, rights, and the Asian American experience.* New Brunswick, NJ: Rutgers University Press.

Bhabha, H. (1994). The Other Question: Stereotype, Discrimination and the Discourse of Colonialism. In *The Location of Culture.* New York & London: Routledge.

Beckwith, F. J., & Jones, T. E.. (1997). *Affirmative Action: social justice or reverse discrimination?* Amherst, NY: Prometheus Books.

Bennett, M.J. (1986). A developmental approach to train for intercultural sensitivity. *International Journal of Intercultural Relations,* 10(2), 179-196.

Blank, R., & Slipp, S. (1994). *Voices of diversity: Real people talk about problems and solutions in a workplace where everyone is not alike.* New York: American management Association.

Bonacich, E. (1973). A theory of middleman minorities. *American Sociological Review,* 35, pp. 583-594.

Brown, C. (1965). *Manchild in the promised land.* New York: Macmillan.

Carr, L. G. (1997). *"Color-blind" racism.* Thousand Oaks, CA: Sage Publications.

Chan, S. (1991). *Asian Americans: an interpretive history.* Boston, MA: Twayne.

Chang, G. H. (2001). *Asian American and politics.* Washington, DC: Woodrow Wilson Center Press.

Chen, G. M., & Starosta, W. J. (2005). Where to now for intercultural communication: A dialogue. *International and Intercultural Communication Annual,* 28, 3-13.

Chen. G-M., & Starosta, W. J. (2000). *Communication and global society.* New York: Peter Lang.

Cheung, K.K. (1993). *Articulate Silences: Hisaye Yamamoto, Maxine Hong.* Cornell University Press.

Chun, K. (1980). The myth of Asian American success and its educational ramifications. *IRCD Bullentin,* 1-12.

Cohen, A.P. (1994). *Self Consciousness: An alternative anthropology of identity.* Routledge.

Cose, E. (1997). *Color-blind: seeing beyong race in a race-obsessed world*. New York: HarperCollins.

Creswell, J.W. (1998). *Qualitative inquiry and research design: Choosing among five traditions*. Sage Publication.

D'Souza, D. (1995). *The end of racism*. New York: Free Press.

Denzin, N. & Lincoln, Y. (1994; 2005). *Handbook of qualitative research*. Thousand Oaks, CA: Sage.

Ellison, R. (1947). *Invisible man*. New York: Vintage International.

Espiritu, Y. L. (1992). *Asian American panethnicity: Bridging institutions and identities*. Philadelphia, PA: Temple University Press.

Fontana, A. and Frey, J. H. (1994). Interviewing: The Art of Science. In Norman K. Denzin and Y. S. Lincoln, (Eds.), *Handbook of Qualitative Research*, p. 361-376, Thousand Oaks, CA: Sage Publications.

Franklin, A. J. (1999). Invisibility syndrome and racial identity development in psychotherapy and counseling African American men. *The Counseling Psychologist*, 27(6), 761-793.

Glaser, B.G. & Strauss, A. L. (1967) *The discovery of grounded theory: strategies for qualitative research*. Chicago, IL: Aldine.

Gordon, M. (1964). *Assimilation in American life: the role of race, religion, and national origin*. New York, NY: Oxford University Press.

Gudykunst, W. B. (2001). *Asian American ethnicity and communication*. Thousand Oaks, CA: Sage.

Gupta, C., Chattapadhyaya, D. P. (1998). *Cultural otherness and beyond*. Danvers, MA: Brill.

Hallam, E., & Street, B. V. (2000) (eds). *Cultural encounters: representing "otherness."* New York, NY: Routledge.

Harris, H. E. (2000). *The perceived influence of culture and ethnicity on the communicative dynamics of the United Nations secretariat*. Howard University Dissertation.

Hune, S. (1998). *Asian Pacific American women in higher education: claiming visibility and voice*. Washington, DC: Association of American Colleges and Universities.

Hurh, W.M., Kim, K.C(1989). The 'success' image of Asian Americans: Its validity, and its practical and theoretical implications, *Ethnic and Racial Studies, 12*, 512–538.

Jackson, R., II. (2003). *African American communication and identities: essential readings*. Thousands Oaks, CA: Sage..

Jackson, R., II. (1999). *Negotiation of cultural identity: perceptions of European Americans and African Americans*. Thousands Oaks, CA: Sage.

Janesick (1994). The Dance of Qualitative Research Design: Metaphor, Methodolatry, and Meaning. In N.K. Denzin, & Y. S. Lincoln (Eds.) *Handbook of qualitative research*. Thousand Oaks, CA: Sage

JanMohamed, A.R. and Lloyd, D. (1990). The nature and context of minority discourse. Oxford University Press

Johnson, F. L. (2000). *Speaking culturally: Language diversity in the United States*. Thousand Oaks, CA: Sage.

Johnston, W. & Packer, A. (1987). *Workforce 2000: work and workers for the twenty-first century.* Indiana: Hudson Institute, Inc.

Jordanova, L. (2000). History, 'otherness' and display. In E. Hallam, & B. V. Street (Eds.) *Cultural encounters: representing "otherness."* New York, NY: Routledge.

Kim, D. Y. (1997). Invisible desires: homoerotic racism and its homophobic critique in Ralph Ellison's *Invisible man. Novel: A Forum on Fiction*, 30 93, 309-329.

Kim, P. S. (1994). Asian Americans in the public service: success, diversity, discrimination. *Public Administration Review*, 54(3), 285-290.

Kuran, T. (1993). A backlash against affirmative action is growing among whites. In P.A.Winters (ed.) *Race relations: opposing viewpoints.* San Diego, CA: Greenhaven Press, Inc.

Kvale, S. (1983). The qualitative research interview: a phenomenological and a hermeneutical mode of understanding. *Journal of Phenomenological Psychology*, 14 (2), 171-196.

Kwong, Pl (1987). *The new Chinatown.* New York: Hill & Wang.

Lee, S. J. (1996). *Unraveling the "model minority" stereotype: Listening to Asian American youth.* Teachers College, Columbia University.

Lee, W.S. (1992, April). *Flipping face like flipping paper: Conflict resolution among Taiwanese students in the United States.* Paper presented at ECA Convention, Pittsburgh, 1991.

Lewis, D. R. (2003). Still native: The significance of Native Americans in the hstory of the twentieth-century American west. *The Western Historical Quarterly*, 24 (2), pp. 203-227.

Lin, M., Kwan, K, Cheung, A, & Fiske (2005). Stereotype content model explains prejudice for an envied outgroup: Anti-Asian-Americans Prejudice. *Personality and Social Psychology Bulletin*, 31(1), 34-47.

Lindlof, T. R. (1995). *Qualitative research methods.* Thousands Oaks, CA: Sage.

Liu, E. (1998). *The accidental Asian: Note of a native speaker.* New York: Random House.

Lowe, L. (1998). The power of culture. *Journal of Asian American Studies*, 1 (1), 5-29.

Ma, R. (1999). The relationship between intercultural communication and nonverbal communication revisited: From facial expression to discrimination. *New Jersey Journal of Communicaiton*, 7, 180-189.

Mascia-Lees, F.E., Sharpe, P., & Cohen, C.B. (1989). The Postmodernist Turn in Anthropology: Cautions from a Feminist Perspective. *Signs*, 15 (1), 7-33.

McWhorter, J. H. (2000). Losing the race: Self-sabotage in Black America. New York: The Free Press.

Min, P. G. (1995). An overview of Asian Americans. In Mind (ed.). *Asian American contemporary trends and issues.* Newsbury Park, CA: Sage.

Min, P. G. and Kim, R. (1999). *Struggling for ethnic identity: narratives by Asian American professionals.* Walnut Creek, CA: Altamira/Sage.

Naber, N. (2000). Ambiguous Insiders: An investigation of Arab American invisibility." Ethnic and Racial Studies 23.1: 37-61.

Nagel, J. (1994). Constructing Ethnicity: Creating and Recreating Ethnic Identity and Culture. *Social Problems*, 41(1), Special Issue on Immigration, Race, and Ethnicity in America, 152-176.

Ogbu, J. (1987). Variability in Minority School Performance: A Problem in Search of an Explanation. *Anthropology & Education Quarterly*, 18(4), 312-334.

Olzak, S. (1983). Contemporary Ethnic Mobilization. *Annual Review of Sociology*, 9, 355-374.

Omi, M., & Winant, H. (1996). *Racial formation in the United States: from 1960s to the 1980s*. 2nd edition. New York: Routledge.

Ong, P., & Nakanish D. T. (1996). Becoming citizens, becoming voters: The naturalization and political participation of Asian Pacific immigrants. In the G. H. Chang (ed.). *Asian Americans and politics: perspectives, experiences, prospects*. Washington, DC: Woodrow.

Orbe, M. P. (1998). *Constructing Co-cultural theory: an exploration of cultural, power, and communication*. Thousand Oaks, CA: Sage Publications.

Orbe, M. P. (2000). Centralizing diverse racial/ethnic voices in scholarly research: the value of phenomenological inquiry. *International Journal of Intercultural Relations*, 24, 603-621.

Park, K. (1996). Use and Abuse of Race and Culture: Black-Korean Tension in America. *American Anthropologist*, New Series, 98 (3), 492-499.

Parham, T. A. (1999). Invisibility syndrome in African descent people: understanding the cultural manifestations of the struggle for self-affirmation. *The Counseling Psychologist*, 27(6), 794-812.

Peller G. (1995). *Critical Race Theory*. NY: The New Press

Petersen, W. (1966). Success story: Japanese American style. *New York Time Magazine,* 9 January.

Sleeter, C.E. (1993). How white teachers construct race. In C. McCarthy & W. Crichlow (Eds.), *Race, identity, and representation in education,* 157-171. Routledge.

Spivak, G. (1988). Can the subaltern talk? In G. Nelson & L. Grossberg (Eds.) *Marxism and the Interpretation of culture*. Chicago, IL: University of Illinois.

Starosta, W. J. & Chen, G.M. (2003). On theorizing difference: Culture as centrism. In W. J. Starosta & G-M. Chen (Eds.). *International and Intercultural Communication Annual* 26. Thousand Oaks, CA: Sage.

Strauss, A, and Corbin, J. (1990). Basics of qualitative research: grounded theory procedures and techniques. Newbury Park: Sage.

Strauss, A. and Corbin, J. (1994). Grounded Theory Methodology: An Overview. In N. K. Denzin and Y. S. Lincoln, (Eds.), *Handbook of Qualitative Research*, 273-285, Thousand Oaks, CA: Sage Publications.

Sue, S. (1993). *The changing Asian American population: mental health policy. In Policy issues to the year 2020*. pp. 79-93. CA: LEAP Asian Pacific American public policy institute and UCLA Asian American Studies Center.

Sue, S., Kitano, H.H.L (1973). Stereotype as a measure of success. *Journal of Social Issues*, 29 (2), 83-98.

Sun, W., & Starosta, W. J. (2002). "Fact-to-Fact" or "Person-to-Person": Expatriate Chinese consider conflict in USAmerica. *World Communication,*30 (2), 24-44.

Sun, W. & Starosta, W. J. (2006). Perceptions of Minority Invisibility among Asian American Professionals. *Howard Journal of Communications*, 17 (2). 119-142.

Suzuki, R.H. (1980). Education and the socialization of Asian Americans: a revolutionist analysis of the "model minority" thesis. In R. Endo, S. Sue, & N. N. Wagner (Eds.) *Asian Americans: social and psychological Perspectives*, 2,155-175. Ben Lomond, CA: Science and Behavior Books.

Sykes, C. J. (1992). *A nation of victims*. New York: St. Martin's Press.

Takaki, R. (1989). *Strangers from a different shore: A history of Asian Americans*. New York: Penguin.

Tuan, M. (1999). *Forever foreigners or honorary Whites?: The Asian ethnic experiences today*. Piscataway, NJ: Rutger University Press.

van Dijk, T. A. (1993). *Elite discourse and racism*. Newbury Park, CA: Sage.

Wallace, M. (1990). *Invisibility Blues: from Pop to theory*. New York: Verso.

Willhelm, S. W. (1979). Martin Luther King, Jr. and the Black Experience in America. *Journal of Black Studies*, 10(1), 3-19.

Wong, P., Lai, C. F., Nagasawa, R., & Lin, T. (1998). Asian Americans as a model minority: self-perception and perceptions by other racial groups. *Sociological Perspectives*, 41 (1), 95-109.

Wyatt, G. E. (1999). Beyond invisibility of African American males: the effects on women and families. *The Counseling Psychologist*, 27(6), 802-820.

Wright, R. (1966). *Black boy*. New York: Harper & Row.

Wright, R. L. (2002). *Issues on contemporary African American issues*. Unpublished manuscript.

Yancy, W., Ericksen, E., and Juliani R. (1976). Emergent ethnicity: A review and reformulation. *American Sociological Review*, 41, 391–402

Zeener, W. (1991). *Minorities in the middle: a cross-cultural analysis*. Albany, NY: SUNY Press.

.

Index

affirmative action, 15
African American, 2, 53, 55
Asian American, 3, 4, 7, 17, 22, 45
assimilation, 23, 35, 44; cultural
    assimilation, 6; social assimilation, 6

Chan, Sucheng, 23
Chang, Gordon H., 7, 22, 23
Chen, Guo-Ming, 26, 74
co-cultural theory, 24
color blindness, 13
Creswell, John W., 25, 26

dual identity, 43
Denzin, Norman, 23

Ellison, Ralph, 1
ethnic group relationship, 57-60, 71
ethno-relativism, 24
European American, 34, 53

Glaser, Barney G., 26
grounded theory, 26
Gudykunst, William B., 23, 76

in-depth interview, 27-28
Invisible Man. See Ellison, Ralph
invisibility, 1, 3, 8, 13, 21, 47, 49, 61,
    72; individual invisibility, 37, 40, 67;

group invisibility, 46, 69; other group
    invisibility, 57; minority invisibility,
    3, 8, 13
intercultural listening, 26

Jackson, Ronald, II, 2
JanMohamed, Abdul R., 15, 16

Kvale, Steinar, 27-28

Lee, Stacey J., 18, 20
Lincoln, Yvonna S., 25
Lindolf, Thomas R., 25, 27
Liu, Eric, 3, 20
Lloyd, David, 15, 16
Lowe, Lisa, 20

mainstream American culture, 3, 5, 44, 68
McWhorter, John H., 2, 77
Min, Pyong G., 3-6
model minority, 20, 49-53, 70

Omi, Michael, 10-13. *See also* racial
    formation
Orbe, Mark, 2, 26, 73, 74. *See also* co-
    cultural theory
otherness, 13

praxis, 30, 61-65

qualitative research design, 25-26

racial appearance, 36
racial awareness, 33; individual racial
    awareness, 33-43; group racial
    awareness, 43-56; other group racial
    awareness, 56-60
racial formation, 10-13
racism, 19
recognition, 47

resistance, 48
reverse discrimination, 13

silenced/muted group,17
Starosta, William J., 24, 26, 74; Third
    Cultural Building, The, 24;
    Intercultural listening, 26
Sun, Wei, 28
Strauss, Anselm L., 26
stereotype, 18, 21, 51

Winant, Howard, 10-13. *See also* racial
    formation

About the Author

Wei Sun holds a Ph.D. in Communication and Culture from Howard University. She is Assistant Professor in the Department of Communications at Bowie State University, Maryland. Her research interests include conflict management in intercultural communication context, cultural adjustment, crisis communication, minority invisibility and media studies. She is a member of International Communication Association, National Communication, Eastern Communication Association and Association for Chinese Communication Studies. She teaches both graduate and undergraduate courses in her specialties at Bowie State University. Her publications have appeared on *The Howard Journal of Communications*, *Intercultural Communication Studies*, and *World Communication.* Her works have been included in several books also.